ALGIERS, THIRD WORLD CAPITAL

ALGIERS
THIRD
WORLD
CAPITAL

Freedom Fighters,
Revolutionaries, Black Panthers

ELAINE MOKHTEFI

VERSO

First published by Verso 2018
© Elaine Mokhtefi 2018

Images reproduced with permission: Gamma-Rapho KO27312-A4;
Magnum, NYC37020; Magnum, PAR111338; Magnum, PAR409361;
Gamma-Rapho, KA10532TER_042; Magnum, PAR356568; Magnum,
PAR167091; Gamma-Rapho, RH080659; Magnum, PAR167078

1 3 5 7 9 10 8 6 4 2

Verso
UK: 6 Meard Street, London W1F 0EG
US: 20 Jay Street, Suite 1010, Brooklyn, NY 11201
versobooks.com

Verso is the imprint of New Left Books

ISBN-13: 978-1-78873-000-6
ISBN-13: 978-1-78873-001-3 (UK EBK)
ISBN-13: 978-1-78873-002-0 (US EBK)

British Library Cataloguing in Publication Data
A catalogue record for this book is available from the British Library

Library of Congress Cataloging-in-Publication Data

Names: Mokhtefi, Elaine, author.
Title: Algiers, Third World capital : Black Panthers, freedom fighters,
  revolutionaries / Elaine Mokhtefi.
Description: Brooklyn : Verso Books, 2018.
Identifiers: LCCN 2018003409| ISBN 9781788730006 (alk. paper) | ISBN
  9781788730020 (united states)
Subjects: LCSH: Mokhtefi, Elaine. | Black Panther Party—Political
  activity—Algeria—Algiers. | Journalists—Algeria—Algiers—Biography. |
  Civil rights movements—Algeria—Algiers—History—20th century. | Algiers
  (Algeria)—Politics and government—20th century. |
  Algeria—History—1962–1990. | Algeria—History—Revolution, 1954–1962.
Classification: LCC DT295.55.M65 A3 2018 | DDC 965.05092—dc23
LC record available at https://lccn.loc.gov/2018003409

Typeset in Fournier MT by Hewer Text UK Ltd, Edinburgh
Printed and bound by Maple Press, York PA

Nous avons vécu tous les âges tous les temps.

—Mokhtar Mokhtefi

Contents

Preface

In December 1951, I boarded the Dutch ship Veendam in Newport News, Virginia; destination Europe. The seas were heavy and the small ship bobbed and tangoed across the Atlantic. It took two weeks to reach Rotterdam, its harbor dizzy with small boats darting in every direction. From there, I took a slow train to Paris. I was just twenty-three.

I had traveled in the States before. I had lived in small towns in New York State, Connecticut, Georgia, and Texas, and in New York City. But Paris was something else. Just six years after the Second World War, the city was still bandaged and suffering from the loss of status and self-respect. It had succumbed to Nazi occupation, but something of its magic was still intact. I discovered a grey city, a northern city, humid with daily rains; a sad place with sparks of genius, with an underlying sense of art, design, and fashion, and a strong belief in its place in history. I felt certain I would imbibe something basic from a world transitioning from the murky depths of war. I would drink at the fountain of the past and be better prepared for life, innocent American that I was.

In the Paris underbelly, however, dramas were being acted out that took some months for me to register and absorb. A subclass and subculture of Algerian immigrant labor was engaging in an existential battle for recognition and freedom. Little did I know when I rented my first room in a cheap hotel on the rue Saint-André-des-Arts, at the edge of one of the most crowded and intense of the North African quarters, how intimate and involved I would become with their struggle.

That the independence of Algeria would then lead me to participate in another fundamental battle—that of the Black Panther Party against the US power machine—was just as far from my imagination. There was no way I could have foreseen that Eldridge Cleaver would arrive clandestinely in Algiers, on my doorstep, and that the two of us would become collaborators.

I lived in independent Algeria for twelve years. In 1974, I was deported after a series of events stemming from my friendship with the wife of the former Algerian president. I have never been back. For years, friends have urged me to tell my story. I have finally taken the plunge. I bear no grudges. I feel no rancor. This is a story with a beginning and an end.

1

Post-War Paris

Paris was not a war-scarred city: it hadn't been bombed out. It was fixed in time, stationary and visibly weary, a city of past grandeur on display in urban castles, monuments, churches, royal estates and bridges, all under gray skies. There was no modern edge. The contrasts with the United States were striking, often chilling, and I was immediately taken. People were small or of medium height, somewhat drab and old-fashioned in look; if high fashion and couture were Parisian, they were not visible on the city's streets. There, women were appareled in straight or, at most, pleated skirts, stockings and sensible shoes. They projected an overall hue of gray or brown. Men wore hats or berets and ties, and everybody shook hands whether they knew you or not; friends and relatives kissed on both cheeks every time they met, which could be several times a day. The masculine working population mostly wore ill-shaped royal-blue cotton jackets and pants. No one spoke English, nor were we foreigners much appreciated for our attempts at their language: "That's not French," was the comment, meaning "You're killing our language and that's inadmissible." On the whole, people were not outgoing or especially friendly. There was a degree of mistrust, even defiance, behind their unsmiling demeanor. On the other hand, the food was great and for me unconventional, daring. I was soon indulging in shellfish, marrow, spices, herbs, game, innards, and an amazing array of desserts, aperitifs and wine. The whole of France closed down from twelve to two for the main meal, always wine-accompanied, either at home or in canteens or restaurants, then went back to work until seven. If you became a regular at a particular restaurant, you were assigned your own red-and-white napkin, kept in storage for you in a pigeonhole along the wall; the same might apply to unfinished bottles of wine. On descending onto the platform of a subway station, ladies in uniform, mostly war widows I learned, punched your ticket. City buses had open-air back platforms that agile travelers hopped onto by lifting a lightly attached chain. Cars were miniature and few; large American cars drew immediate attention, people gathering and commenting in detail on the trappings: the dashboards, logos, hubcaps, upholstery and the rest. Miles per liter was a never-ending subject of conversation.

There were exceptions to similarity and they were notable. My first night in Paris, I sat at a table in a restaurant near the Étoile with my friends Bill Friedlander and Naseem Beg. Imprinted on my memory in indelible ink is the image of a tall, fancifully-dressed woman who strolled by in a long, flowing winter coat and a broad-brimmed hat, all black. As I watched from the enclosed terrace of the restaurant, she lifted her gloved hand to drag on a cigarette through a holder; then, head held high, she released the smoke. She was laughing, detached from the man at her side. I had never seen anyone like her, the epitome of worldliness.

The second unforgettable image I encountered when out walking the following morning. On the Left Bank, in the doorway of a building near Notre Dame, I came across two older

women enclosed in shawls and long dark skirts, round-shoul-
dered, their graying hair swept up into loose buns. They were
talking under their breath with barely a gesture, immobile. It
was my first encounter with the French concierges, lodged in
practically every Parisian building at the time, who carried out
the duties of American building superintendents, but also acted
as quasi-official informants for the police.

There were the cops on the beat, as well—should I even call
them "cops?" Too streetwise a term for the dashing fellows
wearing hard pillboxes with brims and capes that twirled as they
turned and twisted like dancers on the city's streets, surely chosen
for their handsome faces and supple bodies. Nuns were everywhere, too, habits and headgear flowing with the wind, walking
and riding bikes along the avenues, dashes of light blue and white
or all black, very young women with smiles on their faces. Men
of the cloth as well, priests and monks in black or coarse brown,
erstwhile images of Jesus all around the city.

Paris startled me in so many ways. The number of craftspeo-
ple that specialized in small tasks, like the *stoppeuse* who
rethreaded runs in silk stockings and holes in clothing—precise,
eye-wearying work for pennies. Someone called the *rétameur*
repaired holes in pots and other metal pieces. There were shops
that sold only *beurre*, *œufs*, *fromage*, others called *merceries* for
thread, needles, doily and dress patterns. *Bonneteries* cluttered
with bed jackets, underpants, bras, nightcaps, for bedrooms with
little or no heat. Butcher shops that sold only horse meat. Outside
of cafés and restaurants stood little raw-oyster bars, with a dozen
varieties of the astonishing creatures that I had never before
seen, let alone eaten.

The cheap hotels on the Left Bank offered no tubs or showers
with their rooms, so I learned to frequent the *bains-douches*. For

the price of a ticket you received a minute bar of soap and a threadbare towel, but the water was hot. Toilets were located on hotel landings; with toilet paper in one hand, you held your nose with the other. In the 1950s, 84 percent of urban French families had no bathtub or shower at home; traveling by metro at rush hour could be a salty experience.

Making friends was easy enough, first among expatriates and tourists, either at the American Express offices near the Opéra, where we all collected our mail, or in the Left Bank restaurants, where for a few hundred francs, about a dollar, we were fed home-style cooking like none we had ever known, and chatted, often at long tables, bonding for a night, for a week . . . sometimes forever.

Back in the States, I had been totally absorbed in the world government movement. I was director of the student division of the United World Federalists, until politics intervened. It was the McCarthy era and student concern for social justice in the world, the end of colonialism, peace and entente had driven a wedge within the organization that proved terminal. Fearful of McCarthy, who claimed that world government equaled world communism, the student division was thrown out of the organization as too radical. In Paris I contacted the French section of the movement, the International Registry of World Citizens on the place de la Contrescarpe, where Mary Maverick Lloyd of Winnetka, Illinois, and Jacques Savary and Pierre Hovelaque of France distributed world-citizen identity cards and international passports, backed only by their zeal and an official-looking stamp, to partisans of the cause. Garry Davis, a self-proclaimed world citizen who had jettisoned his American passport, was camping out in front of the hall where the Sixth United Nations General Assembly was taking place.

I can never forget Abbé Pierre, in whose ancient Renault Lloyd and Savary and I traveled to a congress of world federalist associations in Belgium. The Abbé, the most popular Frenchman of the time and for decades afterwards, famous *résistant*, advocate of an end to priestly celibacy, knight errant and protector of the poor and downtrodden, wrote toward the end of his life on the problems of sexual desire that plagued him. Unkempt, his beard wispy, his long soutane soiled, he was attentive, soft-voiced, and oh so yearning, his hands abandoning the steering wheel, out of control: humbling, embarrassing me.

Surprisingly, I rarely heard mention of the war that had ended only a few years before. There might be a passing allusion, but it was not discussed or voluntarily recalled. It was taboo except for the occasional reference to the exodus from Paris, when families escaped the capital to find refuge to the south. Even French Jews, who had returned to the city, were disinclined to recount their war experiences. For me, obsessive about politics, this was incomprehensible.

It therefore took me time to put the war in context, to understand how profound was the defeat, how unsettling it remains to this day. The French were a conquered people. They had been occupied by arch-enemies and governed by collaborators. In every neighborhood, within the most patriotic of families, such stains on the past could be found.

Collaboration had perforated and maimed society as much as occupation had. The Resistance had been real, but was significantly magnified and romanticized following the war. It would take decades for the truth of collaboration to be recalled publicly. Marcel Ophüls's two-part film of interviews on collaboration, *The Sorrow and the Pity*, made in 1969, was only authorized for French TV in 1981. The film *Français, si vous saviez* was finally released for public consumption in 1994, twenty-two years after its 1972 production and a half-century after the facts it depicted. As Adam Nossiter has put it: "They were chained to the past."[1]

My "enlightenment" came on May Day, 1952. I'd been living in Paris for several months when I discovered the "lie." It happened as I stood on the rue du Faubourg Saint-Antoine, midway between Nation and Bastille, watching the annual workers' parade.

The day was chilly. At street corners, children and women were selling lilies-of-the-valley, three or four tied in a bunch, gathered at dawn in the woods around Paris. The marchers, however, were dressed for winter, the men with suits and ties, fedoras or berets. The women wore dresses or two-piece outfits over which hung sweaters or raincoats. Their legs were clad in stockings and low-heeled shoes. They walked slowly along the rue du Faubourg Saint-Antoine, heads high with pride.

Banners announced who they were: the electricians' union, the office workers' union, the autoworkers' union, the national teachers' federation, the national council of French women, the students of the African Democratic Assembly. When the central committee of the French Communist Party, headed by Jacques Duclos—wearing a dashing felt hat with a wide brim—came into view, the crowds on the sidewalks cheered and waved.

Many of the banners bore political messages: "Free Henri Martin," "No to the European Defense Community," "Free Zoro Bi-Tra," "Reinstate Family Allocations for Italian Workers," "Social Security for Algeria." France had been waging a merciless war in Indochina since 1946 that the Communist Party and the closely linked trade union confederation (Confédération Générale du Travail, CGT) denounced. I was bewitched by the formidable display of worker solidarity and trade unionism, something I had not known growing up in the United States.

In the early afternoon, as the parade was breaking up, thousands of men appeared out of nowhere, running in formation, ten to twelve abreast. They sped in cadence, arms splayed as they sought to catch up with the vanishing demonstration. They kept coming, more and more—young, grim, slightly built and poorly dressed. They shouted no slogans, carried no flags, no banners. They were Algerian laborers.

They had been scheduled to participate in the parade. Yet at the last minute, the CGT had backtracked on its agreement to include them and then attempted to block the Algerian protestors. I understood why a few weeks later when their leader, the Algerian activist Messali Hadj, was arrested. The CGT had wanted to prevent any demands for Algerian independence at a time when the French government was hell-bent on containing political insurgence against French rule in North Africa. On May 14, as Messali Hadj attempted to address a public meeting in Orléansville, a town in central Algeria, the police opened fire, leaving many wounded and two dead. Messali was whisked away and placed under house arrest in France.

A year later, the CGT performed an about-face and included Messali's organization, the Movement for the Triumph of Democratic Freedoms (MTLD), in its Bastille Day parade in Paris. The French police struck again, opening fire on the Algerian demonstrators, beating and wounding hundreds and killing seven.

That May Day 1952 parade was my first contact with Algeria. The events I witnessed gave the lie to French egalitarianism: the famous motto *liberté, égalité, fraternité* was flipped upside down.

Colonialism and racism stood out as the two pillars of power and supremacy. I was shocked into reality.

I had fallen in love with France even before stepping on board the ship that had carried me across the Atlantic. It was my destiny. It came charged with Zola and Dreyfus, Proust and Flaubert, Cézanne, Degas, Manet. Scott Fitzgerald had adopted France; so had Ernest Hemingway, Richard Wright, Chester Himes . . . Black soldiers in the segregated US Army had been welcomed as equals in France during the Second World War, as they had never been at home. But that May Day, I realized that the French were not colorblind. This was the first in a series of sparks that would ignite my growing rage. Something in me associated those gaunt, olive-skinned men on the Faubourg Saint-Antoine with the darker wayfarers trailing along the dusty roads of the South I had observed in Georgia as a student in the 1940s. I had seen them as desperate and estranged, and they had tugged at my heart.

After that, I became more attentive to the large numbers of North African workers in and around Paris. Just outside the city was a ring of *bidonvilles*, shantytowns constructed from crates, tin, cartons, and planks that were home to thousands of migrants. They spread out under bridges, in trenches or recesses along major highways: rotten, insalubrious hovels, hidden from sight, out of the way of ordinary citizens lest their consciences be burdened.

I had a room for a while near the rue du Pont-de-Grenelle, a street in a workers' quarter leading to the bridge across the Seine on which stands a replica of the Statue of Liberty. Hole-in-the-wall grocery stores and bars catering to a North African clientele lined the street. On warm evenings, men wearing the blue uniforms of France's working class sat on the doorsteps smoking, or leaned into the walls of the small tenement buildings turned dormitories that housed eight and twelve to a room. As I passed, soft voices murmured *bonsoir*.

Closer to the bridge was a *dansing*,[2] a dance hall open on weekends in front of which those same silent workers hung and waited, cigarettes still in hand, but dressed as though for a date. Occasionally, "mixed" couples (North African men and French women) could be seen leaving the hall and strolling off.

Eating in the cheap North African restaurants on the rue de la Huchette, one of the little streets off the boulevard Saint-Michel, became routine. With three American friends, I became addicted to couscous, tagines, and heavy red wine from Algeria. One of the three, Frank, a slim San Franciscan with sallow skin and a drooping mustache, often disappeared down one of those streets, sometimes for an hour, sometimes for a week or two. His girlfriend let me in on his secret life: he was of American and Chinese descent, had been an army pilot during the war, and was running guns for rebels in the mountains of the Moroccan Rif. She showed me a photo of him dressed in a long white hooded djellaba, holding a rifle with two hands.

Work and Play

Life was pleasant enough, but I was running out of money. I had to either find a job or take a boat back to the States. I answered an advertisement in the *International Herald Tribune* and was recruited as a secretary in a Franco-American architectural agency designing bases for the US Air Force, readying France for its role in the North Atlantic Treaty Organization (NATO). The architects and engineers were American, the titular head of the agency was French, and the dozens of draftsmen were architecture students from the École nationale supérieure des Beaux-Arts.

These students introduced me to Parisian bohemia. French schools of higher learning were unapologetically elitist, but these companions were anti-bourgeois, anti-conformist. They acted out their determination to change the social attitudes of a staid, cramped society. One afternoon, the future architect Pierre Ristorcelli, son of a factory owner in Marseille, stood in the middle of the boulevard Saint-Germain, between the church and the Deux Magots café, in tie, shirt, and jacket, but no pants or underpants, and directed traffic for several hours, undisturbed and apparently unconcerned.

Despite the warnings of my nervous employers, I attended the Bal des Quat'z'Arts and other wild events, improvised or organized, emanating from the École. The ball took place in the Salle Wagram, a concert hall on the Right Bank, decorated with piles of hay and a stage on which nude models and students had sex, or played at having sex. It looked real enough to me. Music was provided by a student fanfare of wind instruments that screeched and wheezed through the night. Wine flowed from squat barrel containers.

In the ateliers we had decorated ourselves with all the inventive art of the day. In bras and panties, pancake makeup, colorful tattoos, feathers, and outsized phony jewelry, we made our way through the streets of the Left Bank and crossed the Seine, taking over cafés and restaurants along the way, eating and drinking anything our hands could get a firm grip on. When the night was over, we dragged ourselves to the place de la Concorde and bathed in the fountains, leaving makeup, paint, and bits of costume behind.

I spent my weekends at the *pince-fesses* (literally "ass-pinchers") in the students' ateliers—noisy, heavy-drinking, hands-on dance fests.

As soon as the weather turned warm, I quit the job and took off in a convoy of cars with my new friends for southern France where, on the Côte d'Azur, we improvised as a touring company. With César the sculptor and Paulmard the painter, we put on evening shows in the guise of a film crew in from Hollywood—complete with an American vedette!—beguiling the bourgeois vacationers for our bed and board. I ate my first fresh figs snipped from the tree. We drank cloudy pale-yellow pastis. I adopted the bikini—which the painter Mireille Gouirand and I concocted from a large square cotton scarf by dividing it crosswise in two and adding a few stitches to hold the ends together. I swam in the Mediterranean and visited the Picasso Museum in Antibes as the sea air rolled in through billowing muslin curtains. In those days Sainte-Maxime and Saint-Tropez were unpretentious fishing villages. The beaches of Nice were covered with *galets*, oval-shaped stones weathered smooth by the sea.

I had no idea where all of this was taking me, but I was having a wonderful time. The men and women I traveled with were not necessarily older, but they were more sure of themselves. They seemed to know where they were going. I felt like a child in comparison. What I had not understood was that their lives were carved out in advance. Their manners, work and education were codified by class. Once on a track, there was danger in changing direction. Soon, I began to see that I had a different outlook: I was from a different place. I was freer, I could change tracks.

That careful, calculating mentality also echoed in relationships that we shared. I was fickle and used to changing partners, taking chances. Potluck was an American pastime. My French friends, however, were dead serious. During that whole summer, the men were flirtatious but no one made a pass at me. They had partners, either present or awaiting their return. Instead, I was a comrade. The fortunate result was that I felt the adopted child. We are still solid friends today.

At the end of the summer we split up. I left Nice for Paris by bus, crossing France through small villages on secondary roads. I had the sense that I was traveling through the Old World and imbibing a bowlful of history. The villages and towns resembled what they must have looked like at the end of the nineteenth century: humid, self-enclosed, and silent.

Along the way, I took the decision to hang in. What did I have to go back to? What did I have to lose?

International Conference World

On my return to Paris I enrolled in the Sorbonne, but managed poorly. I started skipping classes and looking up people I had met in the youth and student movement in the US. As my French improved, I was hired as a translator and interpreter for meetings and conferences; people with good working knowledge of two or more languages were in short supply in those years. I began to travel to other cities and other continents: north to Sweden for a youth seminar, south to Rome for meetings of the FAO (United Nations Food and Agriculture Organization). In Bamako, Mali, I interpreted at a student and youth conference. At UNESCO's 1956 General Conference in New Delhi, I was posted with Tunisia's first delegation to an international meeting as an independent country. The delegation was headed by future prime minister Mohammed Mzali.

In 1953, the Eisenhower White House introduced a loyalty oath for all American employees of United Nations organizations. No American could be employed under any condition—not for an hour, not for a day—by a specialized UN agency without presenting a document known as the "clearance." I applied for the famous document but was turned down, no reason given.

In the back of my mind, however, I recalled events that had happened just before I traveled to Europe. In the summer of 1951, I had attended the World Assembly of Youth (WAY) congress at Cornell University, which brought together delegations of young people from all over the world, except the Communist bloc. I was openly denunciatory on the subject of racism in the United States. And our guests, among whom were many delegates from Africa, wanted and needed to know what our politics were. I later heard that FBI agents had come to my hometown of Ridgefield afterwards asking questions about me—specifically, I was told, about my comments concerning "Negroes." Clearly, that was all it took to be blacklisted.

There were, however, ways around the problem. At UNESCO I was paid by the Tunisian delegation, at the FAO by the Italian government. The Paris office of the International Civil Aviation Organization (ICAO) refused to recognize the "clearance" during the years I worked there. Walter Binaghi of Argentina was the president of the organization and held firmly to a policy of independence with respect to the member countries, including the United States.

In Conakry, Guinea, at a meeting of the International Association of Democratic Lawyers, I saw the petty machinations of Cold War politics at first hand. It was played out within the confines of a conference organized and financed by a pro-Communist international organization. The technicians, equipment, and interpreters had come from China, except for a Frenchwoman and me, who were hired by the Guinean government. On the eve of the conference, I was asked to interpret privately for the Guinean minister of justice, who was the French-speaking chairman of the conference, and the head of the Japanese delegation, who spoke fluent English. Their meeting was aimed at coordinating the positions of their delegations so as not to be outmaneuvered by the Communist delegations—and to avoid any condemnation of the United States in the final resolutions.

As the conference proceeded, a draft text on the Korean War that vilified the United States and called for Korean reunification was introduced in committee and passed. In the final hours of the conference, however, the Guinean chairman unabashedly refused to put that resolution to the vote of the plenary assembly. Delegates jumped from their seats in protest. The chairman called for order, to no avail. Losing all composure, waving his arms in an ugly gesture of rejection, he shouted, "Go back to Korea to settle the Korean question!" and stomped off the stage.

The Chinese technicians reacted in a flash, turning off the speakers' and interpreters' microphones, thereby shutting down not only the sound but the conference. As the delegates milled about in confusion and amazement, I watched from my post in the English-language booth as the two American observers in the visitors' section left their seats and exited the hall.

Working from the WAY headquarters in Brussels, I organized the 1960 international congress in Accra, Ghana, Africa's first independent postcolonial state. I also worked on tours for delegates to the newly sovereign countries of Togo, Dahomey (now Benin), Guinea, Senegal, and Mali. I plane-hopped to visit each country, passing through lean-to airdromes onto makeshift runways. Traveling in West Africa at the time was hazardous. Planes were few, while schedules were rarely respected, and reservations were subject to cancellation on a moment's notice. Every trip was an adventure.

Kwame Nkrumah, the president of Ghana, had invited the WAY, but when it came time for the meeting, he had second thoughts: Would he not appear too pro-Western, not sufficiently independent of the two blocs? The invitation was not withdrawn, but contacts with Ghanaian officials turned testy. The delegates coming off the two Super Constellation planes I had arranged were subjected to endless, needless delays at the airport. The Ghanaian personnel with whom I had negotiated became unreceptive. Nkrumah had been scheduled to open the meeting, but sent the minister of social welfare instead, to relay his congratulatory message of goodwill and success. I was witnessing, at close range, the tentative first steps of the new West African countries, the incompetence, the lack of organization, the ambivalence— but also the pride of being on their feet. I wondered about the future.

The meeting was taking place against a background of increasing turbulence on the African continent. The fledgling government of Patrice Lumumba was facing Belgian military intervention in an attempt to destabilize the Democratic Republic of the Congo. With the former colonial army's support, Moïse Tshombe, strongman of Katanga, declared independence for the mineral-rich province. UN armed intervention was being organized and Ghana announced its readiness to participate in Dag Hammarskjöld's effort to maintain the new country's unity. The UN resolution envisaged a surveillance force, without authority to intervene militarily, leading Ghana and a number of other participating countries to later withdraw their contingents on grounds that they served only to entrench an unacceptable division of the DRC. That summer, eleven African countries—including nine former French colonies—became independent. The Algerian war, however, was entering its sixth year . . .

Decolonization was a central issue of the post-war era. The French colonial war against Vietnam had endured nine long years before the final destruction of the French army at Dien Bien Phu in 1954, the same year the Algerian war for freedom from France erupted. The world asked: Had the French not had enough? For the Big Three (UK, USSR, and USA), France was a fading power, adjusting poorly to the new international realities. But President de Gaulle fought hard to convince Eisenhower that France must retain its imperial status and be regarded as a full-fledged partner in directing world politics. After all, wasn't France a veto-holding partner on the United Nations Security Council? Wouldn't her nuclear experimentation in the Algerian Sahara soon endow her with membership in another exclusive club of nations—those possessing the bomb—despite Washington's refusal to supply the expertise?

Algeria was de Gaulle's linchpin, the link between metropolitan France and the former French colonies in North, West, and Central Africa. However, the force of the insurgency in Algeria required French troops (twelve out of its fourteen divisions) that could no longer be counted on to cover for NATO in Europe. In contrast, the United States, while cajoling its erstwhile partner, considered the battle being waged for Algérie-Française as a lost cause, and the sooner it was resolved, the sooner France would be able to fulfill its responsibilities in Europe by bringing the troops back to their own shores.

The Algerian war became the defining issue of the 1950s in Europe. Everyone took sides, and wherever I lived—in France,

Switzerland and Belgium—I became involved, marching in anti-war demonstrations, attending international meetings and discussions, introducing resolutions, denouncing torture. I met Algerian militants and representatives along the road at every stop. At the WAY Assembly in Accra in 1960, it was Frantz Fanon, the Algerian roving ambassador to Africa stationed in Ghana, and Mohamed Sahnoun, the Algerian student delegate.

Together we formed a threesome at the Accra meeting, working to convince delegations to support resolutions against racism and colonialism. We hung out together on the campus and in Accra, unaware that we would all three coincide again on another continent.

By the end of the decade, after eight years in Europe, I was fully immersed in political life. My private life resembled my work life: busy, flipping between one city and another, one task and another: hypermobile, ungrounded. There was no one waiting for me. I was thirty-one, and had not had a serious relationship for years. And so, in September 1960, I decided to go back to the States. I had not been home for four years, although my mother had visited me in Europe in 1954 and again in 1957. Our trips together to Switzerland and Spain and Morocco, to Italy and around France, created a bond that we were both grateful for. She had never set foot in Europe before I moved there. I was at the helm; I did the planning, gave the orders, and did the talking in a cocktail of languages. She was totally dependent on me and we both found that soothing.

2

The Algerian War

I went to New York to see Mohamed Sahnoun, who was studying at New York University. The camaraderie that had brewed between us in Ghana had stayed with me, and I wanted to test it further. As did he. "I've been waiting for you," he said when we embraced at Grand Central Station.

While a student in Algiers, Mohamed had joined a social group active in one of the city's most frightful slums, Hussein Dey. The initiative was launched by Germaine Tillion, the *résistante*, and progressive Catholic priests in the hope of establishing a working relationship with young Algerians. At the time, the initiative had been considered audacious: the European and indigenous populations inhabited totally separate worlds, and the settler population considered intermingling indecent.

In early 1957, three years into the colonial war, the French government turned Algeria over to military command. Everyone associated with the social center was arrested. The Algerians were tortured—men and women—then imprisoned. Upon his release a year later, Mohamed found his way to Lausanne, Switzerland, where the Algerian national student association (UGEMA) was headquartered. He was granted one of the first US National Student Association scholarships for the United States.

I hadn't been wrong. My memories of Accra, where we had shared moments of intense idealism and closeness, had become a longing. We spent our days and nights together, avoiding thoughts of the future.

Nine years had passed since I had left New York. I was more knowledgeable about the world. My politics were clearly to the left: anti-colonialist, antiracist, socialist. I had developed a taste for art and architecture. I knew something about fashion and clothes. I was more sophisticated, but I'm not sure I knew myself better. I still took chances and hoped for the best. I did know, however, that at some point I had to make a decision, buy a plane ticket and go back to my studio in Paris and my work in the international conference world. That was where my life now was.

One day, Mohamed took me to visit the Algerian Office, which handled relations with the United Nations and with the UN delegations for the Provisional Government of the Algerian Republic. That work centered on the annual UN debate on the "Algerian question," a euphemism for "Algerian war" used in deference to France who refused to acknowledge the truth of the conflict, maintaining that it was an internal affair on the level of a local protest movement. Mohamed introduced me to the representative, Abdelkader Chanderli, who showed me around the office and took us to lunch. As we left the restaurant, Chanderli asked if I would be willing to stay in New York and work on his team. The surprise was total, and my reply immediate: "Yes, I would!"

Algerians had been waging political battles against the colonizer since the 1920s, when Messali Hadj, the father of Algerian nationalism, founded the radical independence movement l'Étoile Nord-Africaine (the North African Star). Faced with bans, arrests, and death at the hands of France's repressive forces, Algerians defended and reinvented themselves through the years. They raised new leaders and built new organizations: the Algerian People's Party (PPA), the Movement for the Triumph of Democratic Liberties (MTLD), the Special Organization (OS), the Movement for the Algerian Manifesto (UDMA), the Revolutionary Committee for Unity and Action (CRUA). When all else failed, they trained secretly and took up arms. With unsophisticated weapons—rusty, worn-down shotguns and rifles, bombs handmade from tin cans stuffed with powder—they struck.

On November 1, 1954, All Saints' Day, twenty-two brave fighters launched a series of attacks against French colonial targets across Algeria. Under the name National Liberation Front (Front de Libération Nationale, or FLN), they called upon all Algerian nationalist organizations, all partisans of independence, to join them. They called on France to negotiate. This was the start of a nasty, deadly eight-year war, which pitted a technologically advanced, well-armed European nation (the fourth most powerful military establishment in the world) against a ragtag army of peasants and barely literate villagers.

Minister of the Interior François Mitterrand reacted with force: "Algeria is France . . . The only negotiation is war." And so the repression began. France dispatched thousands, then hundreds of thousands of troops, both conscripted and enlisted. Close to two million Frenchmen took part in the war as soldiers or police. Torture was systematic. Tens of thousands of men and women were arrested on any pretext and subjected to waterboarding (*la baignoire*), electric shocks on the genitals, broken bottles thrust into the anus, and summary executions. For France it turned into a "race war," the ever-burgeoning population their obsession. Children and adolescents—Algeria's future generations—were eliminated, wiped out, shot, starved, maimed.

Tallies of the number of people killed vary: of a population of nine million, it is estimated that between 300,000 and 500,000 died. According to French sources,[1] over two million men, women, and children—one-quarter of the indigenous population—were herded into concentration camps. Their villages, their crops, and their herds were burned and slain. To quote the historian Alistair Horne, the camps "varied from resembling the fortified villages of the Middle Ages to the concentration camps of a more recent past."[2]

On the eve of independence, the 500,000 books in the University of Algiers library went up in flames. The fires were lit by the dean of the university and the head librarian, who fled, along with 900,000 other settlers, across the Mediterranean to France: they torched the books "so as not to leave them for the FLN."[3] In Algiers, Oran, Constantine, the bodies of cleaning women, their traditional robes stained with their own blood, lay in the streets. Official buildings were bombed. The Radiology Department of the Mustapha Hospital in Algiers was demolished. Classrooms were destroyed, and whole schools burned. By the time of independence, 2.5 million children suffered from tuberculosis or rickets. According to the International Red Cross, 50 percent of the population was destitute, hungry, and sick.

What justification could there be for such bloodlust and inhumanity? As of 1955, the first year of the war, torture had become an instrument of France's war, as readily used as the gun. Denial by French politicians and civil servants became standard. I remember having lunch at the home of the secretary-general of the French Senate in the late 1950s, and listening to him declare that "Frenchmen are incapable of such savagery." The archives of the war were closed to the public for thirty years, a period extendable for up to sixty years for those documents involving "state security."

It was only in June 1999 that the French National Assembly voted to define the "events" that took place in Algeria from 1954 to 1962 as "war." In 2017, at long last, France provided the map of the eleven million mines planted along the borders and around the military camps of Algeria during the war.[4]

Algerian Office, New York

The Algerian Office on East 46th Street was an apartment transformed for work. My desk was set up in the former master bedroom, the room farthest from the street, alongside a long meeting table and bookshelves containing literature on Algeria and recent newspapers and magazines, mostly French: *Le Monde*, *France Observateur*, *Afrique Action*, an occasional *France-Soir*, but also the *New York Times* and the *New York Herald Tribune*. Since the "meeting room" was also the "waiting room," I got to meet and talk to everyone who passed through. Abdelkader Chanderli worked in the front office, the former living room.

It was a tiny operation that achieved large, amazing results, even more so when compared to France's diplomatic mission of 93 employees, plus the Washington embassy personnel. The tentacles of war had reached quickly over the Mediterranean divide into the international arena, with conferences, resolutions, petitions, protests, and foreign aid. France's contention that Algeria was an internal French problem, that could be dismissed like some unruly demonstrations, convinced no one. For many observers, the war was won on the world's playing field and at the UN as much as on the battlefield.

The office was within walking distance of the UN, between Second and Third Avenues. I received a *laissez-passer* from the

Tunisian Permanent Mission that enabled me to go in and out of the halls and offices of the international organization: to lunch in the UN cafeteria, order coffee in the delegates' lounge where vedettes of the world's political stage like Golda Meir were holding court, visit journalists' offices, deliver documents to delegation members, or just listen to the debates.

That small office was the official US headquarters of the Provisional Government of the Algerian Republic, the FLN, the ALN (Armée de libération nationale), and all the other hands and feet of the revolution. The French complained often and bitterly to the State Department, even to the White House, about our office's activities, against its very existence. They even objected to Algerians entering the United States on passports from friendly Arab countries. Washington replied that no US laws were being flouted.

Chanderli, a former division head at UNESCO, was an experienced journalist and polyglot who spoke five languages. He was short, bald, and pudgy, a generous man whose charm was enveloping. He organized weekend sorties for our small group of office workers to the countryside, took us out to dinner, or invited us to his apartment where we stuffed ourselves with his wife Franca's delectable Italian cooking. From time to time I was given an envelope with a few survival dollars, not enough to be called a salary. Money was never discussed between us.[5]

Chanderli was assisted by Raouf Boudjakdji, the very, very handsome future ambassador to India and to the UN in Geneva, who would marry Millicent, the granddaughter of William Randolph Hearst. There was something sweet and innocent about Raouf. He was a man devoid of the fire and anger, the dark side, I saw in many Algerians I met. My other colleagues were Marianne Davis, an attractive French-speaking American, and,

part-time, Barbara Malley, wife of the Egyptian-American journalist Simon Malley.

I moved in with Mohamed, into his minute sixth-floor walkup in Greenwich Village. It was here that he and Noël Favrelière,
a deserter from the French Army in Algeria, had been attacked a
few months earlier by an assassin from the Main Rouge (Red
Hand), a terrorist outgrowth of the French police and the settler
population in Algeria. Noël had answered a knock on the door.
Someone had jumped at him with a knife. Mohamed, just behind
him, had pulled Noël back and slammed the door. He had thankfully received only cuts.

Mornings, on my way to work, I picked up the New York
newspapers at the West Fourth Street subway station. The *New
York Times* was our weathervane; how often Algeria appeared on
the front page was a gauge for measuring our progress as players
on the world stage. Over the two previous years, 1958 and 1959,
the Algerian war had featured nearly 200 times. News originated
in Algiers or Paris or through the *Times*'s permanent corre-
spondent in Tunis, Tom Brady, if not from our office.

We wrote press releases, speeches, leaflets. We organized
information meetings for interested groups: non-governmental
organizations accredited to the UN, American student and
community organizations. Ours was a democratic outfit: we all
did a little of everything, from translation and editorials to
running errands to emptying the ashtrays.

The core of our work was with the United Nations. We
contacted and informed delegates and UN personnel so as to
influence the annual debate on the Algerian question. The goal
was to win the largest number of favorable votes on a resolution
denouncing France's colonial war in the strongest possible terms.
This included the treatment of prisoners, torture, violations of

international agreements on war and genocide, and displacement of the population in camps, as well as supporting Algeria's right to independence. France's influence over the votes gradually declined and in 1961, the last session before Algerian independence, the General Assembly voted 63 to 0, with 38 abstentions (the US included), in favor of Algerian independence.

Every Algerian home equipped with a radio was tuned to Radio Tunis or Radio Cairo nightly for news on the UN debate. Algerians who could get their hands on a foreign newspaper or the undercover edition of *El Moudjahid*, the revolution's journal, followed the news out of New York. It was proof that the suffering and sacrifices they endured chimed with world opinion. That France was being accused, disparaged, and censured by dozens of delegates on the banks of the East River was cause for pride and reason to hope.

We also attended cocktail parties and receptions at delegation headquarters. When the Iraqi ambassador to the UN honored the Algerian delegation, I stood three feet from Nikita Khrushchev. There I was, in the same room with one of the two most powerful men in the world. Everyone was taken by surprise; he was the unexpected guest who had come to make a point. It was in October 1960, just after he took off his shoe at the UN and pounded it on the desk in a gesture of ill humor against the Filipino delegate, who had accused the Soviet Union of employing double standards on questions of colonialism.

The Soviet Union had initially supported the French position, in the belief that France was maintaining the United States at bay in North Africa by clinging to its rebellious colony and waging war.[6] The French Communist Party followed suit with a firm stand against independence. The Algerian Communist Party, on the contrary, merged with the FLN by agreement in 1956.

When the Provisional Government of the Algerian Republic, the GPRA, was formed in September 1958 and sought recognition around the world, de Gaulle, obsessed with the war's impact on France's reputation, warned of dire consequences for countries recognizing the Algerian "state" in exile. He put pressure on those responding positively to the Algerian initiative, denigrating some, cajoling and attempting to buy off others. But the GPRA put an efficient set-up in place, with the attributes of a government that commanded respect, whereas French policy at the UN and with its allies was descending into mayhem. In that same month of October 1960, the USSR recognized the GPRA, de facto if not de jure. The Asian Communist countries—North Vietnam, North Korea and China, an early purveyor of arms—recognized the GPRA de jure in its first month of existence. The Soviet Union was, however, also an early supplier under cover of Syria and Egypt. Other Warsaw Pact nations had been providing not only scholarships and training, but arms and munitions for several years.

During this period the Algerian Office saw a stream of revolutionaries who would become the elite of independent Algeria: future ministers, ambassadors, politicians, top-level civil servants. Some arrived as students with American or international scholarships, a few with acute health problems. Others came through on their way to other places, Latin America or Canada. Most came to attend the annual fall sessions of the United Nations: Minister of War Krim Belkacem;[7] Benyoucef Benkhedda, future president of the provisional government; Minister of Information Mhamed Yazid; Mohamed Benyahia, future minister of information and later of foreign affairs; Lakhdar Brahimi, future minister of foreign affairs and UN special envoy to Iraq, Afghanistan, and Syria; Ahmed

Boumendjel,[8] future minister of public works; Ahmed Taleb, future minister of information, of education, of foreign affairs; Ali Yahia Abdennour, minister and president of the Algerian League for the Defense of Human Rights; and others.

They wandered in and out of the office waiting for the committee debates. We took them shopping, and showed them New York. We lunched and dined: Abdelkader often counted on me to enhance their American immersion by taking them to places like Hamburger Heaven or Chock full o'Nuts. We shepherded them to downtown Brooklyn where a woman from Algeria ran a restaurant serving authentic Algerian cuisine. We went to shows, listened to jazz, and, with some, became close friends. Benyahia hung out with Mohamed and me at our favorite Little Italy cafés where poets gathered against a background of Keaton and Chaplin films. The two of us spent an evening with Lakhdar Brahimi at Café Society Downtown, listening to a young, exquisite Miriam Makeba sing, wearing a close-fitting gown, one shoulder bared.

Foreign journalists in New York for the UN debates—Jean Daniel of *Le Nouvel Observateur*, Jean Lacouture of *Le Monde*, Simon Malley of Radio Tunis and *Afrique Action*—dropped in almost daily for information, interviews and gossip, and even to have me type up their articles. It was Simon Malley who gave me some information to process and turn into an article for one of the Egyptian newspapers he represented. He accompanied the request with advice that would guide me every time I sat down at a typewriter in the years that followed: one idea, one central thrust from start to finish. Never stray.

I was dedicated, proud to be part of the unfolding play of Algerian independence. I realized, however, that I had much to learn about politics and political motivation, about discretion and the importance of observation. I apprehended, with time, subtle divisions among the delegates. These fissures became clearer as I learned more about their individual backgrounds, former political choices, and social status. Subgroups quietly revealed those whose political trajectory had evolved from the relatively conservative Friends of the Algerian Manifesto (AML) as opposed to those from the more radical Movement for the Triumph of Democratic Liberties (MTLD), two organizations that had dissolved upon joining the FLN. I grew to be careful, even mistrustful, of my reactions. I taught myself to stop and think.

I was integrating into a society whose rules were not those of my native country, nor of the Western European countries in which I had lived. The place of women, and of foreign women in particular, had to be taken into account. The forms of respect for one's elders, the way one dressed, one's manners, the requirements of religious beliefs and etiquette, while not totally absent from my education, were nowhere as regulated as they were for Algerians. To them, I was an American who spoke French. The fact that I was from a Jewish family did not define me.

Algerians had lived alongside the French in their own land, ignored and despised, robbed and exploited. Racism had become codified in education and politics. The Jews of Algeria were Arabic-speaking neighbors, subjected to the same slights of colonialism as the Muslim population, despite the Crémieux Decree of 1870 which gave them automatic French citizenship, setting them on the road to advanced education and Europeanization. In contrast, the Muslim population was governed by the infamous Indigenous Code, a series of rigid, discriminatory laws. It was the same population separated by religious adherence. French colonialism confined the entire native population to a permanent state of subordination. During the Second World War, Muslim Algeria had shown solidarity with their Jewish compatriots and shielded them. However, the war for independence would change their relationship more than the Crémieux Decree had. In the end, the Jews would reject solidarity and rush to France, and to some degree Israel, to live out their lives. For many of them, it was exile; they, the offspring of the sunbaked Maghreb, would find it difficult to adapt in France. Their tears have never ceased to flow.

I felt comfortable with the Algerians. They were dedicated, affectionate, and generous combatants. I dug their sensitivity. Like them, I saw myself as American, not as Jewish American nor as an American Jew.

The Algerian Office became more than the home for a single independence campaign. Activists from other liberation movements, who wanted to learn how to work with the UN, were sent to us for training. The first to arrive was the representative of an Angolan group, the Union of Peoples of Angola (which in 1962 became the Angolan National Liberation Front), whose president was Holden Roberto. I remember this envoy as, at first, a totally inexperienced young man, overwhelmed by his responsibilities; he sweated and stuttered constantly.

Algeria's initial support of the group was the result of an Algerian delegation's meetings with Patrice Lumumba and Holden Roberto in Accra in 1958, at the first All-African People's Conference. The delegation was headed by Frantz Fanon, who also traveled to Leopoldville for meetings with Lumumba during his short time as premier of the newly independent Congo.

In Conakry in early 1960, as I made my rounds to organize West African tours for the WAY congress to be held that summer in Accra, I was contacted by a small group of Angolans who had formed an organization called MPLA (Popular Movement for the Liberation of Angola), unknown at the time to the outside world. We met in a bare, thatched-roof hut on the outskirts of the Guinean capital, the group's first foothold in Africa. Here I found a handful of silent men around their spokesman, who asked me to press their case abroad. Armed activity inside Angola had not yet begun, but the Portuguese dictator António Salazar had outlawed the new organization and arrested some of its leaders. The group provided me with documents in French and Portuguese that I translated and distributed to UN delegations.

In the summer following that meeting, during the WAY congress in Accra, an MPLA delegate arrived, an impressive young man whom Mohamed and I took under our wing, much to Fanon's annoyance. ("They're Communists," he said.) Once independent, Algeria began backing and training the MPLA in addition to liberation movements in the Portuguese colonies of Mozambique, Guinea-Bissau, and Cape Verde.

It was also in the New York office that some of the first contacts with US agencies and associations took place, through emissaries like Jay Lovestone, Louise Page Morris, Norman Thomas, and a mysterious Mr. Wilson from Washington.[9] They came to talk, exchange information, and occasionally give "advice," which was often ignored. That was the case the day I sat in Abdelkader's office listening to Norman Thomas explain how inadvisable it would be for Abdelkader to speak at the congress of a progressive lawyers' association.

The State Department and the White House carefully continued to follow France's lead. On July 2, 1957, John F. Kennedy had denounced French colonialism in Algeria from the floor of the Senate, attacking President Eisenhower for his "head-in-the-sand" policy of providing arms to France through NATO. He argued that the battle against Communism in the Third World would be lost unless the West recognized that "the worldwide struggle against imperialism, the sweep of nationalism, is the most potent force in foreign affairs today."[10] During the 1960 presidential campaign, our office made a series of attempts to push candidate Kennedy to reiterate his 1957 stand publicly, but to no avail. Privately Robert Kennedy stated that his brother's position had not varied. Once in office, Kennedy also confirmed to Mongi Slim, the Tunisian ambassador, that he stood behind his earlier statement. But never did he repeat this in public.

Nonetheless, conversations were initiated in private. In 1958, Chanderli and Yazid visited the State Department "unofficially" but, following complaints from France, were advised to "stay away." Seen from Paris, the Americans were allies but also rivals, with the means and the desire to wedge their way into North African politics for the long term.

Washington archives reveal several discreet meetings between State Department representatives and Algerian spokesmen. Officially, however, until the eve of independence, no contacts between the United States and the Provisional Government of the Algerian Republic took place. Even then, they were sparing, as the State Department painstakingly debated whether its first meeting with Chanderli should be at the level of assistant secretary of state or undersecretary of state.

Every Algerian who had ever settled in New York found their way to the office: boxers, chefs, bartenders, and a few intellectuals like my friend Pablo (Mahmoud) Boutiba, who was both a doctoral candidate and a bartender. They were all Algerian-born US citizens.

Algerian sailors on merchant ships arriving in New York harbor brought us merguez sausage and contributions collected from crew members. Irish sailors on British ships, supporters of the Irish Republican Army, passed the hat and deposited their take with us.

After the fascist *pied-noir*[11] organization Main Rouge attacked our office, and covered the outside door and walls with vulgar, threatening slogans, one of those boxers, Lahouari Godih, began serving as our bodyguard. We never saw Lahouari fight. He gave us tickets to Madison Square Garden for the night he was scheduled to follow the main bout. That fight pitched welterweight Emile Griffith from the US Virgin Islands against Benny "the Kid" Paret from Cuba. Mohamed and I watched, sickened and helpless, as Griffith hammered Paret to death, the referee standing by and the crowd demanding more . . . until it was too late. He had to be carried out on a stretcher and died in hospital ten days later. Lahouari's match was cancelled. I believe he never fought again.

During spring break in 1961, Mohamed and I drove from New York to New Orleans in an outdated Oldsmobile my father had passed on to me. Mohamed had never been south, and we had never traveled together. We disconnected from our workloads and took to the road. It was a joyride.

We stopped in Atlanta and visited Martin Luther King Jr.'s headquarters, the Southern Christian Leadership Conference. The staff that day was jubilant: Rich's department store (now Macy's) had been integrated. An attempted sit-in, six months earlier at the top-floor Magnolia Room restaurant, had led to King's arrest and his transfer to a vicious Georgia chain gang. His life was in the balance. Harris Wofford, founder of the student division of the United World Federalists, in which I had been active years before, pressured presidential candidate John F. Kennedy to call Coretta Scott King; his subsequent intervention led to King's release from the chain gang. When Martin

Luther King's father came out in support of Kennedy, the Black vote followed suit and tipped the balance in JFK's favor.

As we drove through town after town in Georgia, Alabama, Mississippi, Mohamed became increasingly aware of himself. His hair and eyes were black, his skin olive-tinted, his nose sharp. In the climate of extreme tension that prevailed in those years, I felt him quiver with anticipation. There evolved a picture in our minds of violence and "southern justice." In New Orleans we found a room in a worn-down antebellum home surrounded by tall weeds and wildflowers and wandered about the city, listening to jazz and eating gumbo.

In early June we left for Tunis. While Mohamed attended a student conference, I visited the Ministry of Information and was introduced to members of the staff. I spent a comfortable day with Olive La Guardia Yazid—Mhamed's American wife and Mayor Fiorello La Guardia's niece—and their baby Hediya, whose crib rocked with the occasional boost from Olive's foot. The sun poured in through the curtained windows of the villa and patterns formed on the floor. I wandered through the souk and bought a small rug for my parents. Mohamed said I should have bargained for it. We went swimming on an empty beach along the Mediterranean. Recognizing Algerians among the people on the streets, in the cafés, rendezvousing with comrades from an earlier life, we felt we were not far from "home." The atmosphere was warm, expectant.

East Africa

Before returning to New York for the next UN session, I went to Dar es Salaam to interpret at the 2nd Pan-African Youth Seminar.

Invited by Julius Nyerere, whose leadership took his country—then called Tanganyika, now Tanzania—from colonial status to independence before the end of 1961, the conference brought together representatives of independent African countries and struggling liberation movements, in particular from Algeria and the Portuguese colonies. Nyerere was an educator and trade union leader, aptly called Baba, father of his country.

During the seminar a trip to Kenya was organized for a group of delegates and I to meet Jomo Kenyatta, the pan-Africanist and anti-colonialist, who had just been transferred to a hamlet close to Nairobi by the British authorities, following years of prison and house detention in a remote part of Kenya. Kenyatta had been accused of leading the Mau Mau rebellion of 1951, although no proof was ever found. He would become Kenya's president upon independence in 1963, and remain in power for fifteen years.

The house was a single-floor square building, surrounded on all sides by a wire barrier guarded by armed British soldiers. A short distance from the barrier, great crowds of Kenyans created a slow, circular path around their leader's quarters, swaying and chanting day and night. Many had trekked from distant mountains, and wore on their backs the skins of animals from their regions. Beyond the lines of people I could see the rolling hills of Kenya's famous tea plantations.

Kenyatta invited the group of young Africans and me, the interpreter, into the compound. Accompanied by his daughter Margaret, he spoke to each of us in turn, inquired as to where we were from, and thanked us for the visit. He then led us to the barrier and, speaking through a megaphone in Swahili to the crowds of well-wishers, invited them to welcome the Algerian delegate, who made a short speech in French. I interpreted into

English the delegate's conviction that their two countries' struggles for independence would soon be victorious.

Before our group left Kenya, we were taken by jeep to the Nairobi National Park, a stone's throw from the city. The park was closed to visitors, but we were allowed in as special guests. The jeeps rolled through lush, wild, undulating terrain, traveling side by side with herds of antelopes, zebras, gazelles, elands, impalas, and ostriches. We saw a lion in his lair, monkeys everywhere, rhinos—and not a single human being.

Frantz Fanon

When Frantz Fanon landed in Washington in October 1961, he was terminally ill with leukemia. As soon as our office learned of his arrival, we took responsibility for his needs. He never made it to New York.

Fanon was born and raised on the West Indian island of Martinique, then a French overseas department (a territory whose relation to France was on the order of Puerto Rico's to the United States). During the Second World War, Fanon managed to escape the island's Vichy regime to enlist with de Gaulle's Free French Forces. He was shipped to North Africa, where he received his first impressions of colonial Algeria while awaiting transfer to Europe. Wounded in action at Colmar near the German border, he was awarded the Croix de Guerre. He returned to Martinique in 1945, finished high school, then left for Lyon, France, where he entered medical school, specializing in psychiatry. He also studied philosophy and was involved in theater. Here he wrote his first book, *Peau noire, masques blancs* (*Black Skin, White Masks*, 1952).

Fanon was passionate about everything he did, from psychiatry to racial politics to soccer. In medicine, he was trained by François Tosquelles, a French Catalan in the vanguard of European institutional psychiatry. In 1953, Fanon was named resident psychiatrist at the Blida-Joinville Psychiatric Hospital in Algeria. Here he discovered a world of alienation: treatment consisted of massive doses of soporifics, lobotomies and other psychosurgical procedures. The hospital was located miles from the city. The patients were locked up, emotionally and physically. Everything contributed to keeping the inmates on the outskirts of society.

Not too many years before Fanon's arrival, the hospital contained structures that included "pits" (*fosses* in French) in which the inmates were crowded to receive food thrust at them from an upper deck. The half-starved men and women in these pits battled each other for morsels of rotting meat and stale bread. The buildings were circular; when not in the pits, inmates were kept in single cells above, barely large enough for their bodies to lie. Though they were no longer in use when Fanon arrived, the buildings still existed at least into the 1960s. I learned of them from Élisabeth Dubreuil, a Swiss psychologist who was shown their remains just after independence.

Although Fanon practiced shock treatment, he eschewed straightjackets, chains, and even walls, while introducing group therapy, ergo-therapy, music, art and sports therapy. For him the hospital had to constitute a world, a social structure in which the patient played an active role. He studied the cultural life of the surrounding Algerian villages and began a transformation of the institution. An Arab coffee bar was built inside one of the pavilions. Muslim holidays were celebrated. Concerts of Arab music, as well as sessions with traditional storytellers, were organized.

The patients wrote and edited a newspaper. A football stadium was built that exists to this day.

"Psychiatry is politics," said Fanon. He never ceased examining, studying and tackling the wrongs he saw before him. Later in Tunis, where he set up a psychiatric day center, he experimented with the idea that patients should not be separated from their milieu, the home environment being part and parcel of their treatment.

After the war for independence broke out in November 1954, Fanon came into contact with the Algerian Liberation Army and began providing medical and psychiatric aid, as well as shelter, to the freedom fighters. In 1956 he resigned from his medical post. In an open letter addressed to Robert Lacoste, the resident-general of Algeria, he declared:

> If psychiatry is the medical technique that aims to enable man no longer to be a stranger in his own environment, I affirm that the Arab, permanent alien in his own country, lives in a state of absolute depersonalization ... How absurd was the idea to want, whatever the cost, to maintain certain values at a time when the absence of law, inequality, the multiple daily murders of human beings have been raised to the level of legislative principles ... The events in Algeria are the logical consequence of an abortive attempt to decerebrate a people.[12]

Lacoste subsequently deported Fanon from Algeria. So the doctor and his family made their way to Tunis, where he joined the Algerian provisional government headquarters and immersed himself in a variety of roles: as staff writer at *El Moudjahid*, the FLN newspaper, and as psychiatrist and head of a day clinic for

Algerian freedom fighters and war victims. He lectured to officers of the Algerian Liberation Army at Ghardimaou on the Algeria–Tunisia border. Fanon's rise in the Algerian hierarchy was phenomenal—especially considering that he was neither Algerian-born or raised, nor was he Muslim.

In December 1958, Fanon headed the Algerian delegation to the All-African People's Conference in Accra, a short-lived but politically powerful organization. It was there that he met and developed close relationships with Patrice Lumumba from the Congo, Holden Roberto (alias Rui Ventura) of Angola, and Félix Moumié of Cameroon. In 1959, he was named the first Algerian ambassador to Ghana. It was there that I met him.

On that day in August 1960, I was walking across the university campus in Accra on my way to the assembly hall and was stopped by a group of four men, three of whom were dressed in dark wool suits and ties; they looked stifled and incongruous under the tropical African sun. The fourth man, Fanon, was wearing light-colored pants and a short-sleeve white shirt, with his jacket under his arm and no tie. He stepped forward and in basic English asked where the World Assembly of Youth congress was taking place. I caught the accent and answered in French, leading the way. He and I spoke, making a connection immediately. He told me later that his first thought was that I was French. When he realized I was not, he was relieved: we could empathize.

The other men followed in silence and I left them at the entrance to the hall. We all shook hands, but no introductions were made. They attended the congress session and, except for Fanon, were gone the next day. To me, their silence and appearance were evocative of the underside of the war, dark and treacherous, and unremittingly clandestine. I later learned that the group had been investigating the possibility of opening a southern front in the war against France, through Mali and the Algerian Sahara. Arms were already traveling that route, leaving the port of Conakry, wending their way through Mali to Tamanrasset and Ain Salah on the backs of camels and men.

Fanon had a long face, a strong, wide jaw, and deep-set, probing eyes. He was short, his body taut. The overall picture was of intensity, a man in a hurry and driven. As an official observer at the WAY congress, Fanon was invited to address the delegates. Mohamed Sahnoun represented UGEMA, the Algerian national student association. The two ensured that a strong resolution condemning France and supporting Algerian independence was passed unanimously. WAY had been at the vanguard of the fight against colonialism since its founding in 1949. When the organization came out in support of Algerian independence, the French national youth council condemned its stand and withdrew from membership.

The day Fanon spoke to the conference, he revealed his roots as a psychiatrist: he read through a number of case histories from his newly published book, *L'an V de la révolution algérienne* (published in English as *A Dying Colonialism*), on the effects of war, poverty, and racism on Algerians he had treated. Losing patience as Fanon went from one case study to another, Sahnoun grabbed the microphone from him and brought the assembly back with a bang to the war for independence, to the need to support the struggle and condemn France.

Sahnoun, Fanon, and I spent hours in the conference hall and on the campus together, pushing for progressive resolutions on Palestine, South Africa, China, agitating for the end of colonialism and the formation of an entente. We were bound by a commitment to African independence and, beyond that, to the anti-imperialist struggle. We visited Fanon's Algerian embassy—no more than a small apartment. I was struck by how spartan it was, how clinical in appearance.

We couldn't have been more different. Mohamed was sharp, quick to react; Frantz relentless and analytic. I was the willing, admiring apprentice of both. Along with Maurice Mpolo, the militant Congolese minister of youth, in uniform, who represented President Patrice Lumumba, they stood out among the delegates. They had put their lives on the line for freedom and justice. A few months later Mpolo would be executed alongside Lumumba.

One night Fanon and I went dancing. A Ghanaian photographer focused his camera on us. Frantz caught him on the edge of the dance floor, and warned him to destroy the photo (it appeared nonetheless in an Accra newspaper a few days later). The FLN had placed a boycott on all French cigarettes. When I shared my Gauloises with him, we became partners in guilt, breaking the ban together.

He once asked me what I wanted in a relationship. When I answered, "To put my head on someone's shoulder," he was adamant: "*Non, non, non*: stay upright on your own two feet and keep moving forward to goals of your own." His words would come back to me often, and I have repeated them to others in need of that advice, as I was at the time.

On his return to Tunis from Accra, in the fall of 1960, Fanon announced to his colleague Marie-Jeanne Manuellan that he was ready to dictate another book—it was to her that he had dictated his previous work, *L'an V*. This one would be called *D'Alger au Cap* (*From Algiers to the Cape*) and draw on his travels in Africa. Marie-Jeanne remembers that conversation well. Fanon, his wife

Josie, and Olivier, their son, were having dinner with her family: "Fanon didn't look well. His skin had a greenish cast," she told me.

Two days later, Fanon arrived at the Manuellans' again, waving a sheaf of little papers. "I've got a good one for you," he announced. "I've got leukemia." And added quickly: "But I'm going to fight it."

"With what?" Marie-Jeanne asked, in shock.

"With the cortex!"

Throughout dinner both families sat grimly, but Fanon kept talking as usual about the war, politics, his time in Black Africa. At the end of the meal, he picked up a rotting apple from the table, twirled it, and declared, "This apple doesn't look good. It's leukemic."

How to save Fanon became the concern of everyone in his entourage and in the offices of the provisional government. France was out of the question. Arrangements were made for him to go to the Soviet Union; Josie and Olivier accompanied him. All seemed to go well. Fanon returned from Moscow jubilant. He had gained ten pounds; his blood was normal. The Soviet doctors gave him another five years. Enough time for new cures to appear.

In the afternoons, Fanon "spoke" his text to Marie-Jeanne, who wrote it down fast with a pencil on large sheets of white paper. He paced the floors and held forth. He never went back over his words: "His sentences flowed all by themselves to the rhythm of his steps around the room. He never sat down. He had no notes in hand." She typed up the sheets and returned them at the following session. She never retyped pages; as far as she knows he made no changes, or minimal ones. And so they worked for close to six months. Leukemia was never mentioned again between them.

In August 1961, the book finished, Fanon went to Rome for an historic three-day meeting with Jean-Paul Sartre. Simone de Beauvoir and Claude Lanzmann, her lover and Sartre's colleague at *Les Temps modernes*, were also present. It was Lanzmann who transported the text of what had become *Les damnés de la terre* (*The Wretched of the Earth*) to François Maspero, the progressive Parisian publisher.

According to Lanzmann, Fanon talked non-stop of the Algerian revolution, of the revolutionary qualities of the soldiers in the "interior" as opposed to the politicians in "outside" Tunisia. He analyzed for them the situation in Angola and in the Congo, where his friend Lumumba had just been assassinated. "The lumpenproletariat of the cities and the poor, illiterate peasantry will take up arms and transform the world," said Fanon. Over and over he stressed the importance of armed struggle for the future of Africa and for the healing of the individual African. Sartre listened, fascinated.

Two months later, Fanon arrived in Washington on a weekend, alone and deathly ill. The disease had reemerged. How he managed to get from the airport to a hotel in the city was a mystery, even to him. He thought it was the end: he demanded that the hotel find him a nurse. The management resisted, but finally yielded when they realized this man might be dying. On October 10, with the nurse's help, he was able to make his way to the National Institutes of Health in Bethesda, Maryland, where arrangements had been made for him to be hospitalized.

I have read in several accounts of Fanon's American destiny that it was the CIA that managed his transfer. The insinuation that Frantz Fanon could have been duped and conveyed by the American spy agency is infuriating. It was normal procedure for Washington to be apprised of his need for treatment at the government hospital in Bethesda, and for the embassy in Tunis to authorize the visa. The contact had to have been initiated by an official representing the GPRA, someone of stature. Fanon may have been critically ill, but his head functioned perfectly. It could never have accommodated the CIA in any shape or form.

No one had accompanied the dying man, and our office was not informed of his arrival until after the fact. Being the only person at the Algerian Office who had ever met Fanon, I became one of two main contact persons, visiting him in Bethesda regularly. Throughout his stay at the hospital, Frantz remained lucid, rapidly perceiving who among his visitors believed in his recovery and who did not; his discourse changed accordingly. On one occasion a Protestant minister came to his bedside, offering help should he be the object of racial discrimination. Fanon snapped back that he could take care of himself, thank you.

Fanon missed Tunis and the offices of the revolution. He missed his comrades, *les frères*. Once, when we were alone in his hospital room, Frantz rose from his bed, sat straight up, and, turning to me, said: "*Ce n'est pas une mauvaise chose de mourir pour son pays.*" ("It's no bad thing to die for one's country.")

When Josie and Olivier arrived in Washington, I took Olivier, who was six, to New York to stay with Mohamed and me, far from the hospital room. We showed him around New York, went to Central Park for rides on the carousel, and rode up to the top of the Empire State building; we took the ferry to Staten Island. Our friend Boutiba gave him a camera to record his experiences.

The day I took Olivier to New York, he asked me to write my name on the frosted window of the hospital room, then he set about copying it. Frantz commented, "He's transferring."

A few days before he died, Fanon received the first copies of *The Wretched of the Earth* containing Sartre's lyrical, passionate preface, which many deem Sartre's finest writing. For Fanon it brought back their meetings in Rome. While Fanon was at death's door, Sartre "was sparing himself," he recalled, by begging off in the evening to retire to bed.

Claude Lanzmann was in touch with a French doctor who had introduced a new means of fighting leukemia through the renewal of the entire blood system, with some success. The doctor in question was on his way to the United States and would visit Fanon. His verdict: "Too late." Fanon died on December 6, 1961. He was thirty-six years old.

In his memoir, published in 2009, Lanzmann states that Fanon was dead by the time he himself arrived in Washington; since I met Lanzmann at Frantz's bedside and heard him speak of the upcoming visit of the French doctor, I have to conclude that his memory is fading. Lanzmann stayed in Washington a few days, saw Fanon, then left for Los Angeles. When he returned, Fanon had indeed died.[13]

Lanzmann joined us in New York and booked into the Hilton, the same hotel as Josie and Olivier. He told us extravagant tales of *"mauvaises rencontres "* (bad encounters) in Los Angeles that he blamed on his *"nez juif"* (Jewish nose). A tough-looking man had shouted anti-Semitic slurs at him through the open window of his rental car when he stopped for a light. The driver then tried to force him off the road but Lanzmann managed to elude him.

Josie lingered in New York, hanging out with us for several weeks. She gave me a long, multicolored, swinging skirt that Frantz had liked. *"Il t'a beaucoup aimée,"* she said. ("He was very fond of you.") Josie and Frantz had met at a movie theater in

Lyon. He watched her as she stood in line to buy a ticket, then followed her in and sat down beside her. She was petite, with a pretty, round face, thick dark hair, large brown eyes, and well-designed lips—*à croquer* (good enough to eat), the French would say. She had a way of speaking under her breath, with short sentences that suggested you were only being given a ladleful, that there was much more in the pot. She evoked mystery and sex.

Josie remained politically involved after Frantz's death, and stayed on in Tunis. After independence, she and Olivier moved to Algiers, where she worked as a journalist in the national press. She supported Boumediene after the coup d'état in 1965 but, as she once told me, "I've never been known for betting on the right horse."[14] During the liberation war, Frantz also had backed Boumediene and the "frontier army," as opposed to the Algerian government in Tunis.

Algerians have reservations about Fanon's writing. Mohammed Harbi, the leading Algerian historian, sums these up in his 2002 afterword to *The Wretched of the Earth*: "Our disagreements stem from the generative role he assigned to the peasantry, his belief in the unanimity of the national conscience and his approach to the religious phenomenon." Given that he spent his life essentially among agnostics, Fanon was incapable "of measuring how derisory a place the Enlightenment occupied within the Algerian cultural sphere." Harbi adds:

> Fanon took from L'Internationale, and made his own, the idea: "*Du passé, faisons table rase*" (Of the past, let us make a clean slate). [But] we cannot understand his basic tenet if we bypass Marx's contributions . . . [Fanon] wasn't satisfied with a purely economic analysis of imperialism . . . and

attempted to show that the true wretched of the earth, those exploited absolutely, are the colonized.[15]

Harbi concludes: "The case against the West cannot be circumscribed to a single option, solely that of nationalism: it is universal aspiration that is the motor."

The Wretched of the Earth has become required reading, a manual of revolution, for militants around the globe. For Huey Newton and Bobby Seale of the Black Panther Party, it outlined the exemplary, transformative philosophy of violence required for the victims of a racist society.

3

Moving to Algiers

I had never been to Algeria, but I was "algerianizing." I was in love with Mohamed. How could I not be part of the new country that had so affected my life?

On March 19, 1962, a ceasefire came into effect following drawn-out negotiations in Évian. De Gaulle was a stubborn bargainer. He had refused to negotiate sovereignty with an Algerian government, even a provisional one, as two equals: the Algerians participated in the talks as the FLN.

In April, 91 percent of the French electorate approved "self-determination" for Algeria by referendum, with enough of a majority to indicate that the people had had their fill of war. On July 1, the population of Algeria was asked: "Should Algeria become an independent state cooperating with France according to the rules defined in the March 19, 1962, declarations?" The result was overwhelming: six million people came out to vote for independence; 16,534 voted against.

Mohamed and I left for Paris shortly after the ceasefire went into effect, then went on to Lausanne, Switzerland, to the wartime headquarters of UGEMA, the Algerian national student organization. We didn't tarry, however. Mohamed was anxious to go home, to find his mother and two sisters. There was trouble in

Algeria, especially in the large cities of Algiers and Oran. He feared for his family. The *Organisation de l'armée secrète* (OAS), a fascist militia composed of settlers and military personnel, was terrorizing the population, killing with impunity men and women from every walk of life. They scourged the cities and country-side with fire, blasts, and bullets in a final burst of barbarity. But the war was over; France was pulling out. The terrorists, too, would have to take to the road.

Mohamed left for Algiers. Meanwhile I visited the headquarters of the Algerian delegation to the Évian peace negotiations. Mohamed Benyahia took me on a tour of the premises they occupied, the conference rooms, and the press room where Krim Belkacem issued his daily progress reports. I lunched with the delegates in the dining room at the communal table, recognizing once again the directness and informality of Algerian protocol, a reflection of their basic egalitarianism.

I went back to Paris to wait for the situation in Algiers to settle down, assuming that the vote on July 1 and the proclamation of Algerian independence would put an end to the violence. But another crisis was brewing. In June, at the end of a congress of Algerian leaders held in Tripoli, Libya, the GPRA fell apart. The struggle for power, placed on the back burner for years, steamed, and then boiled over.

On one side were members of the provisional government under Benyoucef Benkhedda, on the other were Ahmed Ben Bella and Colonel Houari Boumediene, head of the liberation army. The former group retired to Tizi Ouzou, a city to the east of Algiers and the Berber capital of the country, and the latter to Tlemcen in western Algeria, along the Moroccan border. Though the split has been described as ideological, it was mostly a battle of persons and power. In between the eastern and western group headquarters were a number of military regions taking positions for or against either camp.

On August 30, Boumediene's army began its march on Algiers. It possessed superior firepower, which he used with impunity against any opposition. Men who had spent years battling the French military now faced their own kith and kin. Civilians who tried to stop the fighting were fired upon. In Algiers, thousands marched to the Forum in the center of the city, screaming, "Seven years of war— ENOUGH!"

Benkhedda and former members of the GPRA entered Algiers in an attempt to claim their legitimate right to govern. On September 4, Ben Bella made an appearance in Algiers; on September 9, Boumediene led his army into the city. The Ben Bella–Boumediene dyad took charge. These events had a lasting effect on Algeria's future. Force and heavy-handedness, rather than the ballot box, became the essential tools of government.

In September I joined Mohamed in Rome, where he and Claude Sixou, Algeria's sole aeronautical engineer, were attending a meeting of the UN's International Civil Aviation Organization—the first international conference attended by representatives of independent Algeria. The three of us drove to Naples in the smallest Fiat in existence and took the boat to Capri for a long weekend among the bougainvillea and Aleppo pines. We climbed to the top of the island to take in the view of its undulating hills, the grand sea, and the Italian coastline. At the end of the conference, Mohamed and I went by train to Florence, then Venice. We found a room in a bed and breakfast next to the Ducal Palace. From our window we looked over Piazza San Marco, the church bells and crowds of pigeons our companions for several magical days. We walked into the Venice International Film Festival, sat down on the floor in the aisles and watched

Pasolini's *Mamma Roma* with Anna Magnani, and Zurlini's *Cronaca Familiare* with Mastroianni. As simple as that.

We parted again. I went to Paris, Mohamed back to Algiers. He would let me know when it was safe to travel to Algeria.

Algiers

Towards the end of October 1962, I arrived on a plane from an era long past, a heavy, slow-flying Breguet double-decker. Every seat was taken. The man next to me introduced himself: Abdelhamid Benzine, journalist with the Communist daily *Alger Républicain*. His response was wide-eyed amazement when he learned that I was American and had worked with the FLN during the war. We were total strangers, but forever after we would greet each other with the warmth and recognition of refugees who had come home from exile at long last.

After disembarkation cards were distributed, I saw that most of the men on the plane were handing them, along with their French identity documents, to the few who had taken out pens and were completing their cards in their own hand. They were Algerian workers returning from France: illiterates all. I would participate in a similar experience every time I flew from France to Algiers. Even my mother, who spoke not a word of French or Arabic, somehow filled out travelers' disembarkation cards on her trips to Algeria.

Night had fallen by the time the plane landed. People were milling about on the tarmac, the reception committee for those who had come to celebrate the anniversary of the November 1 launch of the Algerian Revolution. At the foot of the gangway, a man came forward to embrace me. It was Nourredine Abrous, whom I had known as a student in the States. He had enrolled at the University of Pennsylvania on one of the first American student grants to Algerians, and played soccer with a professional team during the final years of the war. I knew that he had been studying in Toulouse when Algerian students went on strike in May 1956. He was later imprisoned for his activities in the FLN. Nourredine was now part of the new Ministry of Foreign Affairs.

I was directed to a bus filling up with representatives of African liberation movements who had arrived on the same plane, heads of organizations from the Portuguese colonies and the ANC of South Africa, as I remember. We quickly made contact and introduced ourselves during the ride into town. We remained pretty much in the dark, however, until the bus approached the Hôtel d'Angleterre, our destination on the rue Ben M'hidi, formerly rue d'Isly. We had arrived in a modern-looking southern European–style city. Near the hotel we could see two large buildings in a neo-Islamic style, the central post office and a department store. Only the next day did it become clear that Algiers was two cities.

It is built on the side of a mountain that slips into the Mediterranean. Its beauty is startling, its evolution over time clearly visible. Beginning at the western edge, intimate, mysterious neighborhoods, bathed in whitewash over many centuries, have lent the city its name of *Alger la blanche*. This is the Casbah, moving from a lower level of timeworn mosques upward through winding stairways and passageways, famously recorded in the film, *The Battle of Algiers*. At its base the Place des Martyrs, a vast open space above the sea long marred by an outrageous statue of the Duke of Orleans on horseback; visible there throughout the colonial era, it was shipped back to France following independence.

Going east we find the beginnings of the "European" city, with five- and six-story buildings enhanced by shaded arcades, then a pleasant, small park with benches and trees alive with starlings in the evening. Two main thoroughfares follow the path of the sea to the central post office, the imposing neo-Arab building that is the focal point of downtown Algiers, before turning upward on another busy commercial street. Continuing up the hillside is a mesh of winding byways with villas and government buildings, and beyond that, I believe, a proliferation of new highways and unseemly high-rise housing projects. I have not set foot in the city in many decades, but I am told that today the Casbah with its interlocking buildings and rooftops has begun to crumble.

Among the men representing their liberation movements for the anniversary celebrations were poets Viriato da Cruz and Mário de Andrade of the Angolan MPLA, as well as President Agostinho Neto and Lúcio Lara; Eduardo Mondlane and Marcelino dos Santos of FRELIMO in Mozambique, Oliver Tambo and Johnny Makatini of the South African ANC, and Sam Nujoma of SWAPO in Namibia, men who played vital roles in the history of their countries. We got to know each other well. We gathered for meals at a little restaurant on the ramp that led to the lower streets just above the sea. We attended receptions in the old Ottoman palace, plays and concerts around the city. We walked in the Casbah, exchanged tales of the various struggles, and felt kinship: we were fellow militants and the future was ours. The Algerians had done it and so could they.

The celebrations were grandiose: tens of thousands of veterans, women, youth, students, and athletes paraded alongside soldiers of the newly named Armée Nationale Populaire (ANP). Representatives of seventy nations were present. I listened to the congratulatory speeches and my heart filled with emotion. Here and there I ran into Algerians I had met in New York, as well as French radicals I had been in contact with in the past. The euphoria was liberating. The troubling events that had brought Ahmed Ben Bella to power were passed over, though on occasion I was reminded that for some their anger was undigested. As one Algerian friend put it: "Ben Bella thinks he discovered America."

Mohamed was away when I arrived, on a mission to Addis Ababa for the deliberations preparatory to the launch of the Organization of African Unity (now the African Union). As one of the few English-speaking officials at the Ministry of Foreign Affairs, his assignments multiplied, and he was rarely in town. Nevertheless, within a matter of days, I knew I was in Algiers for the long term. The experiment to create a new socialist country from the impoverished colony, the tremendous task of building a state respected in the international arena, was daunting. My gut told me that I would settle here, whatever my future with Mohamed. I would have to find living quarters and a job.

With my friend Mohamed Benyahia, with whom I had bonded in New York, and his comrades Jacques Charbi, Aline Moussaoui, and Mahieddine Moussaoui, I moved into a well-maintained villa with a garden in the exclusive Paradou section of Hydra, above the city. The villa was empty, but not unfurnished. The former inhabitants, whose name was Savon, had left everything behind: furniture, bedding, dishware, silverware, supplies, even clothing, rain shoes and umbrellas. Theirs had been a hurried exit, along with almost a million other settlers, in the final weeks of French rule. The leaders of the new country called for them to return, to live and work in "their" country, but they weren't listening. They were in France, lining up for indemnities from the French government.

I call them settlers because I have no better word. They were not foreigners, in that most were born on Algeria's soil. They were no longer Europeans, though the majority had come from Europe generations before. They were functionaries, low-level employees, small-business people, soldiers, policemen, professionals, and technicians. Some did "settle" on land stolen or seized from the native population over the course of history. What I know is that they were callous, racist, cruel, and ignominious. They held power in their greedy hands and lived the "good" life. They represented the white world. There were few exceptions.

Our little group in Hydra had no car; local transportation was close to nonexistent and taxis were scarce, so we started looking for places to live in town. An elderly Frenchwoman who had refused to join the exodus was loaded with keys to abandoned properties in the European sector. She led us to a completely furnished three-bedroom apartment on the rue Didouche Mourad, one of the two main business streets of Algiers. The furniture was dark and dreary, but solid. The former owners had intended their stay to last a lifetime. This now became our home.

Benyahia had been secretary-general of the provisional government in Tunis under Benyoucef Benkhedda, and part of the Algerian delegation to the peace negotiations with France that ended the war. Frail, hardly more than a pile of bones, light-skinned with pale green eyes that squinted incessantly, he was known for his intelligence and discretion. He had studied law but refused to capitalize on the fact. When a delegation of NGO representatives visiting Algerian headquarters in New York inquired about his personal itinerary, he replied, "I'm an Algerian, no different from every other Algerian fighting for our independence."

He was a gentle, generous comrade and housemate. The apartment that we shared became the nightly meeting place for his friends and former colleagues as they waited for the new government to settle in and provide roles, jobs, and salaries. Nonetheless, he was marked as a major player in the Benkhedda provisional government, which had been thrown out of power by Boumediene and Ben Bella. It took some months, but those who had opposed them were gradually absorbed into the power structure, Benyahia included. It was he who introduced me to Djamel Kesri (better known by his nickname, Nehru), head of the National Office of Algerian Tourism (ONAT), who gave me my first job in Algeria.[1]

In time, the elderly Frenchwoman with the keys found me a large one-bedroom apartment with two balconies and a view of the sea.

Work

People shifted from one job to another with astonishing alacrity. My experience was typical of the time. After a few months at the tourist authority, I transferred out, literally from one day to the next, to become assistant to Cherif Guellal, press and information advisor to President Ahmed Ben Bella. I shared an office with him at the Palais du Gouvernement. We had been introduced at a reception; when he heard me speak, he asked, "Where are you from?" "New York," I answered, and we exchanged a few words in English. A few days later, Guellal appeared at the ONAT office and asked me to come work with him.

I was ready to move on. The tourist office was located in a former Ottoman palace in the lower Casbah, a dream location with a majestic courtyard fountain surrounded by marble tiles and stately tiers recalling other times and other pleasures, but there was no heat during the icy winter of 1962–63. Many of the staff had been intelligence or counterintelligence agents with the provisional government in Tunis. They had been parked at ONAT for the essential purpose of receiving a salary while waiting to be called to other posts. These were men used to double-play, double-talk, and conspiracy theories. We twiddled our thumbs, tried to be friendly, and chatted about the future of Algerian tourism. Would it be tourism for the masses or for the elite?

But there were no tourists, not then nor for many years to come. However, I did get a taste of power politics à l'algérienne. A few members of the staff—Francine Serfati and the poet Colette Melki, well-known Algerian-born FLN militants—decided that the Office should unionize, and put up an announcement for an organizational meeting and election of officers. As quickly as the poster went up it was taken down. Rahmoune Dekkar, national head of the UGTA, arrived in person with a crew to appoint those who would thenceforth represent the agency's workers. The spontaneous notice posted by my colleagues was declared "illegal." No meeting or activity ever followed.

Receiving foreign journalists at the Government Palace became my job, providing information and making appointments for them. The organs they represented were well known: Italian Radio and Television, *France Observateur*, *Le Figaro* and *Le Figaro Littéraire*, *Combat*, *L'Express*, the *New York Times*, TIME, Reuters, UPI . . . I clipped the press and created archives of topics of interest. All unofficial correspondence in English arrived at my desk. I imitated Ben Bella's signature on his official portraits and sent them out on request. It was a puffed-up signature with exaggerated, ballooning Bs; I would later see it as an unflattering reflection of his persona.

Improvisation was the byword. When in March 1963 Guellal learned that the king of Morocco, Hassan II, would be the first official visitor, complete with entourage and trappings, he asked me to outline an arrival protocol—as he considered the newly formed Protocol Office at the Ministry of Foreign Affairs inept. I rewound the film of my memories of newspaper and newsreel presentations of official arrivals in various places in the world and came up with a program. To my satisfaction, I saw that it was followed to the letter, complete with the little boy and the little girl, children of martyrs (*chouhada*) of the liberation war, presenting bouquets to the king.

Improvisation was not only my prerogative; it was nationwide. The great master of improvisation, Ben Bella, also became its slave and victim. He launched new national projects every day, but neglected the measures required to implement them; he created offices and agencies and committees that functioned in name only. Agrarian reform, infrastructure, economic development, housing programs were announced in glowing terms to a beguiled population but rarely saw the light of day. Faced with opposition or conflict, he either caved or strong-armed. One by one, revered leaders of the revolution were dismissed, or resigned. He turned to lesser personalities, made bargains, created parallel political structures. He ordered arrests, and allowed torture.

Ben Bella was popular, he was eloquent, he was attractive; but he had little education, and was overly conscious of his image. Power and increasing adulation isolated him from a truthful examination of events. They provided him with an excessive belief in himself, and a concomitant suspicion of his partners and colleagues.

Within six months, Guellal was named ambassador to Washington. He asked me to accompany him but I chose to stay in Algiers, where everything was brand new—or so it seemed. There were no professionals to speak of, no multilingual cadres, few educated people. Out of a population of nine to ten million, there were but 1,500 Algerian university students and some 500 graduates to manage the country. Fifteen hundred others were studying abroad on scholarships, many of them in Soviet-bloc countries. There were no trained technicians. The French administration had pulled out, leaving little behind. Algeria was an overwhelmingly rural society of poor people, over 90 percent illiterate, who had accomplished the awesome feat of bringing the fourth-greatest military power in the world to its knees.

I was not alone. Several thousand foreigners, partisans of an independent Algeria, arrived from France, Tunisia, and Morocco during those first months of the new country. Many had worked with the FLN during the war as *porteurs de valises* (suitcase carriers), transporting people, arms and money for the revolution. There were men who had lit out or gone underground when they were called up for military service in France, even a few deserters from the French army. Many were highly trained: doctors, engineers, technicians, teachers, professors, lawyers. They were called *pieds-rouges*, a clever if unflattering term, placing them in opposition to the *pieds-noirs* who had fled the country. They were idealists who would build a new world; visionaries whose consciences told them they had to come.

In addition to these brave individuals, countries that had provided unswerving support for an independent Algeria during

the war cooperated with the new government by sending special-
ists, above all medical teams: Yugoslavia, Cuba, China, Bulgaria,
Egypt, Syria, Lebanon, Soviet Union and others. They became
indispensable in a place where the hospitals and clinics had not
only emptied out of personnel in the months preceding independence but suffered from a lack of equipment and medicine. In
addition, these teams had to face the language problem. How to
convert French into the languages they spoke, even summarily?
Algerian Arabic, the only idiom in which the majority of the
population could explain their state of health, took more time
and patience to understand. More than once I accompanied my
friend Zohra Sellami and her brother, who was epileptic, to a
Chinese clinic along the coast. We were astounded by the personnel's devotion to the job of giving the population back its health,
the number of patients they handled daily, the quality of service,
and their gentleness.

Now, in 1964, with the arrival of a conservative director of the
president's cabinet, it was thought unseemly for an American
woman to be employed at the presidential level. I was transferred
to the State Secretariat, headed by Mohammed Bedjaoui, future
member of the International Court of Justice. No one replaced
me at my former post.

I was hardly qualified to write laws. I had no legal background,
and English was not required. I appealed to Ben Bella's chief of
staff, Ahmed Laidi, who made a phone call that whisked me away
to Algérie Presse Service (APS), the government's national
press agency, located in one of the small streets separating the
Casbah and the European section of the city. There I became,
literally, the English desk, as well as one of the daily op-ed writers. The French-language press published my articles partially or
fully with frequency. There were special high moments when the

French press, including *Le Monde*, did the same. I never had a byline.

In 1968, I moved to Radio-Télévision Algérienne (RTA), where I wrote and directed three weekly radio programs devoted to national and international events. For large international meetings I organized daily broadcasts in English for delegates. One of my most memorable interviews was with Pelé, the Brazilian soccer star, whose condemnation of the American war in Vietnam I prompted and recorded.

Two years after I arrived in Algeria, Mohamed and I said goodbye to each other. He had become a diplomat and world traveler whom I only saw on his stopovers in Algiers. Our life together was reduced to the occasional weekend drive in the countryside. When he could sit on the couch in my apartment and describe a woman he'd met in Tanzania "whose skin was like silk," I knew we were doomed. "I think it's time to call it quits," I said. He was surprised but didn't object. I handed him his coat and walked him to the door.

We occasionally ran into each other at meetings, in the halls of a government building, even years later in Paris when he was the Algerian ambassador to France, and were always pleased to see each other. There remained some of the old complicity, but no desire. In my head are snapshots that, put together, become a film. What remains are good memories. I had come to Algeria with him, but not only for him. I had espoused a cause and taken the consequences.

When, sometime later, he married an Algerian woman, he let me know. I found that strange. He felt he owed it to me, whereas I was sure I was my own responsibility, no one else's. I was a happy camper, with friends in several circles, among Algerians and foreigners. I did not have a full-time partner, but I enjoyed a number of interesting experiences. I felt like a well-fitting cog in the machine of Algeria's reconstruction. On a deeper level, I had found a home.

And I felt so at home that I took the potentially fateful decision to apply for Algerian nationality. At the time, dual nationality was a no-no for the American administration. About a year after filing, I received a stock letter informing me that my request had been denied, no explanation given. Seen from today's distance, I realize that I was fortunate.

City Life

Algiers closed down at nightfall. Aside from the Cinémathèque, run by a group of progressive French and Algerian cinephiles— as exciting as anything like it in Paris or New York—nightlife was on a dimmer. Several fine restaurants specialized in either French or North African cuisine, and along the coast were some that served spectacular seafood, but most of us had salaries that didn't allow for frequent trips in their direction.

Stores along the main commercial streets were unattractive and ill-stocked. Even the former Monoprix displayed meager, left-over merchandise in its largely empty shelves and display cases. It would be several years before a walk down rue Didouche Mourad became a shopping excursion. I believe the first expression of home-grown fashion was named Yasmina. On the other hand, visits to the lower Casbah were immediately satisfying. Available there were the traditional products: handwoven baskets and mats, pottery, dresses and scarves, djellabas, haiks, swaddling and baby clothes, as well as second-hand goods left behind by a population in flight.

I spent most evenings and weekends, when I wasn't working, with friends and colleagues *en famille*. On leaving the office, we moved to a midtown bar for drinks and tapas: platters of sautéed anchovies or sardines, sea snails, olives, slices of roast pepper, seasoned lima beans, deposited on the counter and consumed for the price of a drink—then to someone's home for collective cooking. My specialty was Southern fried chicken.

I bonded with people in my building—Simone and Mohamed Rezzoug and their children Leila, Amir, and Hichem, *mon petit amour*—where there was always a place set for me to share in Khadra's extraordinary cuisine. Khadra had been born in a Saharan brothel and grew up a slave. When, on independence, her French owners hightailed it across the Mediterranean, she came north and found work as a cook and nanny. Also in our building was Elisabeth Misteli, the Swiss *coopérante*, a charming and dedicated psychologist, with whom I shared Sunday trips to the country and picnics in Bainem Forest or on the mountain at Chréa.

I developed tremendous affection for several courageous Algerian women: Yamina Belkacem, both of her legs torn off when the bomb she was carrying detonated off-schedule, who was light enough for me to carry in my arms and set on the passenger seat. Nassima Hablal, a war heroine, tortured by the French military at the infamous Villa Susini.[2] Nassima, too, was a splendid cook who showed me how to prepare snails, drowning them in flour in a large jar while they emptied their guts, an unpalatable sight but an amazing dish.

North African cuisine is one of the world's finest—the use of herbs and spices (ras el-hanout), the mixture of sweet and savory, stews slowly simmered, meats on the grill or the spit, homemade flatbreads, rich desserts blending honey and almonds and anointed with rose or orange-blossom spray, all enticing and educating the palate; and, of course, every variety of couscous. During Ramadan, I often joined colleagues at the end of the day's fast. At the APS, it was spectacular: not a soul remained in the newsroom. The world could come to an end, but no one in Algeria would have been informed: we had all headed for the restaurant across the street. The tables were stationed one next to the other in long lines; plates of chorba, a delectable vegetable soup with bits of lamb, awaiting us. The early arrivals sat with spoon in hand, anticipating the boom of the cannon announcing that it was the time to feast and celebrate. Some colleagues stopped in the street first to smoke a cigarette.

As a journalist, I was on the invitation list for official receptions at the Palais du Peuple and at the embassies of Vietnam, North Korea, China, Sweden, even the Soviet Union. I attended soirées at the homes of "in" groups revolving around Cherif Belkacem or Mohamed Benyahia. I spent time with my soulmates at Prensa Latina, Paule Santiago and Americo Nunes. On weekends, I would load up my Austin Mini for the beach at the Club des Pins or Fort de l'Eau for a meal of lamb's head (*bouȝelouf*), seafood, and salads at the long tables lining the streets near the sea. I introduced my visitors from overseas—Pierre Ristorcelli, Yves Antoine, Cynthia Horn, Manolo Jiménez, William and Mary Lloyd, as well as American radicals from Liberation News Service and *The Guardian*—to those pleasures, as well as walks in the upper and lower Casbah and visits to the crafts museum and the art museum that housed the works of Racim, the famous miniaturist.

My mother visited me several times. We drove to the great tourist sites: the Roman ruins at Tipaza celebrated by Albert Camus, the Mausolée Royal de Maurétanie, a huge funereal monument dating from the Numidian period (ca 200 BCE) to Timgad, a Roman city on UNESCO's list of historic sites. We would trail up the steep, winding roads of mountainous Kabylie to buy handmade cloisonné jewelry at Beni Yenni.

From time to time, a few of us would take off for a weekend in Ghardaïa, the eleventh-century capital of the Mzab, whose striking architecture evokes settings from the Bible or the Quran. Or we would travel the coast to an empty beach near Béjaïa and an old hotel on the corniche, the pink laurel outlined against the blue of the Mediterranean.

Zohra Sellami, my journalist friend, and I covered the long swing from one Saharan oasis to another, one date-palm grove to the next, exotic names evoking adventure and legendry: Bou Saâda, Laghouat, Ghardaïa, Ouargla, Touggourt (where we slept on the desert sand), El Oued (constructed entirely of linked white domes), Biskra. In the Aurès Mountains, one of the most impressive landscapes imaginable, we walked among the date palms, were encased by the canyons, and climbed the reddened, darkened slopes. We stood on the Ghoufi "balconies," absorbing the beauty and listening to the trills of descending streams.

I was not lonely. I even found time for the occasional romantic interlude, if not an abiding love or a lifetime partner. I was gradually perceiving how rigid were the norms of this society with respect to sex, love, and marriage. As a rule, men traded freely in love and sex but returned to the family for marriage. Here was the feminine domain par excellence, within which there was little sympathy for the foreign woman, if not outright disdain. Brave was the man who dared circumnavigate this homegrown barrier of stone.

While working at the APS, I gained my one claim to fame: a role in Gillo Pontecorvo's *The Battle of Algiers*. The film was being shot just a few streets away from the APS headquarters. An assistant came seeking extras for a press conference scene, the one in which a French colonel presents Larbi Ben M'hidi, the freedom fighter (*fellagha* in French parlance), to the press. I appear in that film of films for at least thirty seconds (!), clearly visible in the lower right-hand corner of the screen.

I was more frequently in demand to translate or interpret at international conferences, for TV interviews, and for the minister of foreign affairs, Abdelaziz Bouteflika. When President Ben Bella attended the founding conference of the Organization of African Unity, Bouteflika called on me to translate his speech into English prior to his departure. In it, Ben Bella predicted that the OAU charter would remain a dead letter unless the new organization concretely supported the continent's liberation movements with arms, money, and training. He created a sensation at the conference with his down-to-earth appeals for unity and freedom and his denunciation of the colonial powers: "Let us all agree to die a little . . . so that the people still under colonial rule may be free and African unity may not become a vain word."

In August 1963, President Gamal Abdel Nasser of Egypt arrived in Algiers. He was welcomed as a hero by tens of thousands of cheering Algerians who packed the downtown streets eager for a glimpse of the great Arab leader—one of the finest, most loyal supporters of their independence struggle. The evening of a reception and dinner for him at the Palais du Peuple, I sat at a long oval table with members of the Egyptian entourage and their Algerian counterparts. At one end of the table the Algerian chauffeurs, guides, and other nonpolitical personnel were dining with us. The Egyptians couldn't believe their eyes: here was democratic behavior they were ashamed to say did not exist in their country.

One visiting dignitary I interpreted for was President Julius Nyerere of Tanzania. Ben Bella took him to see a large farm on the fertile plain outside Algiers. Using three fingers Ben Bella held up a big, tawny, speckled apple, harvested in the fall and being treated for shipment to Europe: "*Julius, cette pomme est pour vous.*" The estate was managed by former farm laborers under a national agricultural self-management program, called *autogestion*, that ensured the Algerian people's control over all enterprises of whatever sort, including farms and buildings, left vacant by the European settlers. Ownership had been transferred to the Algerian people, but no one slept in the former proprietor's bedroom. A pile of pills still awaited Borgeaud, the exiled lord and master, on the nightstand next to his unoccupied bed.

Between seven and eight million acres of land, practically every industrial enterprise, as well as from 200,000 to 300,000 houses and apartments came under Algerian self-management control. The March decrees, as they were called, represented the cut-off date after which Algeria became the legal operator of the "vacant" effects of their former owners. They established the details of management by committees elected by the workers to run the estates, the mines, and the industrial enterprises. These were revolutionary measures modeled on similar experiments in Cuba and Yugoslavia. My own one-bedroom apartment became a *bien vacant*. I paid my rent (roughly thirty dollars a month) to the city authorities.

The transfer of property, unfortunately, was only one step in the healing process. The underdevelopment resulting from colonialism had been founded, as elsewhere, on racism and inequality, with the goal of taking over the country's resources and destroying its culture. The regeneration sought would require decades of hard work and enlightened leadership.

Algiers soon became a hub for liberation and antifascist organizations in the sixties. I came to know exiles from Spain and Portugal, opponents of the military dictators Franco and Salazar, as well as others from Brazil, Argentina, Venezuela, and Central America, political opponents as well as representatives of guerrilla movements. Every imaginable liberation organization had an office in Algiers, from the National Liberation Front of South Vietnam (the Vietcong) to the ANC, SWAPO, FRELIMO, the MPLA, student hijackers from Ethiopia, and Palestinian liberation organizations.

A number of those organizations sought me out for translation and interpreting services, especially those with English-speaking backgrounds. When Oliver Tambo, founder of the ANC with Nelson Mandela; Joshua Nkomo, the trade-union leader and head of the Zimbabwe African People's Union, a father of his country; or Sam Nujoma, a father of his country of Namibia, arrived in Algiers, I was sure to get a phone call. The South Africans invented a name for me in one of their languages— something on the order of "lifesaver."

When a group of seven Ethiopian students, young opponents of Haile Selassie's regime, arrived at my office at the Ministry of Information and stood around my desk, I felt moved to see a group of comrades who had succeeded in a revolutionary act but were in danger of losing their way. They had hijacked a plane to Sudan whose authorities bundled them off to Algiers, a city for which they were unprepared. Their plan had been to make their way to East Germany or China. I helped them with accreditation as well as translation, and introduced them to other English-speaking militants and refugees.

Life was exciting and eventful. I was the fly on the window, looking in, beating its wings.

Coup d'État

The People's Democratic Republic of Algeria, the largest country in Africa, had arrived in the world in 1962, delivered from the womb of French colonialism and war: underdeveloped despite appearances of modernity. After 132 years of French rule, there were 500 university graduates out of a population of nine million. It was a rural society, over 90 percent illiterate. Close to one million settlers had left on independence, leaving the country stripped of technicians, teachers, medical staff and the rest. The "appearances of modernity" were many: road and railroad networks, partially modern cities, a French-speaking elite, a mixture of traditional and European dress, cafés, theaters, national radio and television. We were too willing to believe and to excuse, naïvely perhaps, the populist discourse of the one-party system, the FLN. We didn't want to be told it wasn't the path to democracy. However, the glory of nationhood was not sufficient to reverse systems put in place during the liberation war by individuals versed in intrigue and machination, who rode into power on the backs of the people's army.

On the morning of June 19, 1965, I drove through the city to work. The air was still, the streets strangely quiet. Tanks were stationed at the main intersections and there was no traffic. Was this part of the set décor for *The Battle of Algiers*? I had thought that the shoot had wrapped up and the film crews were gone.

I parked the car in front of the APS office. From colleagues standing on the sidewalk, I learned that a coup d'état had occurred in the early hours of the morning. "Boumediene's ousted Ben Bella," someone said. Houari Boumediene, minister of defense: the man who had put Ben Bella in office, the man who, in 1963, Ben Bella had named his successor and for whom he had created the post of vice president. "The army must play a political role," he had exclaimed at the time.

"Is Ben Bella dead or alive?" I asked. No one knew.

Inside the agency, people were milling around in shock. Mid-morning, an official from the Ministry of Information arrived in the newsroom to make an announcement: "None of this concerns us. We're just little people. Go back to work." Around noon, the national radio began airing military music and the Algerian national anthem, but no statements were broadcast.

We "little people" had, just yesterday, heard Ben Bella's thunderous voice cry out that, contrary to rumor, he and his minister of defense were together like two fingers of the same hand. "It's the foreign press," he declared, "that is spreading rumors of a conflict within the revolutionary leadership of Algeria. We are more united than ever!"[3]

My question received an answer: he was alive, under guard, and unavailable.

As soon as night fell, I joined the demonstrators—students, young people, even children—on the main thoroughfares near the central Post Office. We were doused by water hoses and blinded with tear gas. Military vehicles bore down on us. Unprepared, with not even handkerchiefs to protect our faces, we screamed and we ran. I could hear cries of "*Yahya Ben Bella!*" "Ben Bella president!" "Down with dictators!" against a background of rhythms drummed on the sides of cars stationed on the streets. We came out again on the following five or six nights, until the crowds were dispersed. We numbered in the hundreds the first few nights, a few thousand at the end. The protests were weak and ineffectual; we were powerless.

Demonstrations in Oran in western Algeria and Annaba in the east were larger and more violent. The French press reported that over a dozen people, including some women, were killed in Annaba. Not even their sacrifice produced a mass eruption. On the other hand, there were no public signs of support for the coup's leaders, either. In most regions, the population received the news of Ben Bella's arrest and his replacement by Boumediene with indifference.

By the third evening, Prensa Latina, the Cuban press agency, had received the text of a major speech by Fidel Castro denouncing the *golpe*. He furiously assailed the leaders of the coup, accusing them of "fratricide," his venom aimed in particular at Foreign Minister Abdelaziz Bouteflika, "because—let no one doubt it—this mastermind of the coup is not a revolutionary but a man of the right who is known as such . . . an enemy of socialism, which means an enemy of the Algerian revolution." He recalled that Ben Bella, "with nothing to gain—and no hope of any material benefit—had come to Cuba braving the imperialists' wrath in those fateful days" of the Cuban missile crisis of 1962, defying President Kennedy by leaving Washington for Havana to embrace the Cuban leader.[4]

In 1963, when Algeria was faced with invasion by Morocco over a question of borders, Castro lost no time in coming to Ben Bella's aid. In secret, he sent two planeloads of Cuban soldiers and two Cuban merchant ships across the Atlantic carrying men, his best Soviet arms, a battalion of tanks, and 5,000 tons of sugar. The Cubans were ready for battle, awaiting their orders, when the dispute was resolved through direct negotiations between the two sides.

My friends at Prensa Latina, Paule and Americo, loaded up my car with copies of the speech, and Paule and I spent the night distributing it to the local and foreign press and embassies. The next day, two guards were placed on twenty-four-hour duty outside the agency, which continued to function regardless. A few weeks later, the guards disappeared as they had come, with no warning or explanation.

How to interpret the lack of public reaction? Was it fear of the military? Was it because national entities such as the FLN, the national trade union, or the youth, student, and women's organizations had issued no call to resist the takeover? The national radio and television stations were occupied and soon began broadcasting messages in favor of the newly formed Revolutionary Council, headed by Boumediene. The press and APS were throttled.

The general line was that nothing had changed except for one man. "Personal power" was the culprit. Several explanations for the takeover have since been put forward by the pundits. The one most usually cited is the bad blood that existed between Ben Bella and Abdelaziz Bouteflika, leading to Ben Bella's demand that he leave the government. Another explanation, also plausible, is the pact between Ben Bella and the incarcerated opponent of the regime, Hocine Aït-Ahmed, a highly respected leader with a large following, notably in the Berber region. Following their agreement, he was scheduled for release. It was then that Boumediene made his move. Aït-Ahmed remained in prison until his escape over a year later.

The initial reaction on the part of organizations and individuals known for their mistrust of the military was to question Boumediene and his entourage, and to attempt to negotiate the future. A month later, an opposition movement, the Organisation de la Résistance Populaire, emerged. Composed of students, youth and political personalities, it became the target of the regime's wrath and within weeks its leaders were jailed.

Certain well-known figures went into hiding or were arrested and tortured: the historian Mohammed Harbi, leaders of the former

Communist Party, political personalities and government ministers known as close allies of Ben Bella. Henri Alleg, the famous author of *La Question*, managed a discreet getaway. A number of foreigners, Algeria's *pieds-rouges*, lit out—some in fear of reprisal, others in condemnation of the coup. Various reports mention assassinations.

Like many functionaries in Algiers, I was critical of Ben Bella and his regime. His decisions were arbitrary; his word was law. There was an arrogance about him, as if he alone knew the truth of the Algerian people and was qualified to represent them—"I am the sole hope of Algeria," he once stated—even though it was well known that the last person to get his ear usually came away with the prize. He became adept at pronouncements, at "besting" others, as he did with René Dumont, the renowned French ecologist, upbraiding him publicly for not believing in Algeria's "exceptionalism."

The details of governing slipped by him. In 1964, the country's leaders met to elaborate the Charte d'Alger and solemnly adopted "self-management" as the basic form of organization of the economy and the society. How to implement that fundamental decision never became Ben Bella's prime agenda. That it resonated well, at home and internationally, sufficed. His concern was with individuals and power.

A gradual realignment of the country's political forces had come about in the three years since independence, under three general groupings: the military and secret police, the progressives, and the religious networks. Under Ben Bella, Algeria's stated democratic and humanitarian ideals were thwarted regularly with arrests, torture, and banishment. Certain leading lights of the struggle for independence, including Ferhat Abbas, the former president of the provisional government in Tunis, had become openly critical of Ben Bella, only to find themselves in confinement in the Sahara. Others, like Hocine Aït-Ahmed and Mohamed Boudiaf, plotted his overthrow and mounted a guerrilla insurgency in the mountains. Ben Bella was accused of despotism, his contradictions highlighted. Since the press was prompt to exercise self-censorship where national issues were concerned, information about and criticism of the regime traveled via the grapevine.

Now, overnight, yesterday's partisans had rejected Ben Bella. The street found no new leaders to support; most feared that the change the coup had wrought would amount to nothing more than one despot exchanged for another.

But hope remained that one day everything would be put right. And we all went back to work.

4

Meeting the Black Panthers

In summer 1967, I represented Algérie Presse Service (APS) at the meeting of the Organization of Latin American Solidarity (OLAS) in Havana. This was a conference of progressive political parties, organizations, and representatives of Latin American guerrilla movements for the purposes of expressing solidarity, coordinating aid, and defining goals for the struggle. I traveled to New York—stopping to see my parents in Ridgefield, to whom I breathed not a word about my destination—and then to Mexico City, where a visa and ticket awaited me at the Cuban embassy. At the airport, all passengers boarding the Cuban aircraft were corralled into a special hall and photographed. It was like being in a police lineup. Every passport was stamped *Salida de México para Habana.*[1]

In Havana, I rendezvoused with Josie Fanon and her son Olivier. We spent the next six weeks taking part in the July 26 anniversary celebrations of the Cuban revolution, participating in the OLAS conference, and visiting the island. The spirit on the island was "up": progressive and proud. Che Guevara had disappeared two years earlier, but the news of fighting in the Bolivian mountains that made headlines during the OLAS meeting led many of us to imagine that Che was leading another country into revolution. (Alas, the tide very quickly turned; in October he was captured and executed.)

Josie and I connected with the Algerian delegation and the chargé d'affaires. Diplomatic representation between Cuba and Algeria, downgraded since Fidel ranted against the Algiers *golpistas* in June 1965, was not reset at the ambassadorial level until some time later. I sent articles nightly—at least on those nights that the wind was blowing in the right direction—by short-wave radio from the OLAS conference to the APS receptors in Algiers. Josie was in Havana as the special envoy of *El Moudjahid*. She wrote two articles at the beginning of the conference, then decided that my daily transmissions were sufficient for the Algerian media; why duplicate? I continued to transmit nightly under my name, but the articles appeared in *El Moudjahid* as the work of "special envoy J. Fanon" or "special envoy of Algérie Presse Service," with no name attached. We only understood that I had been undercut when we returned home to Algiers. I wasn't happy. The tendency in the press was to avoid foreign names, unless they were those of celebrities, or to 'Arabize' them to camouflage the shortage of qualified Algerian journalists. It was a practice that grew silently and that everyone felt obliged to accept.

For the first time, the celebration of the launching of the Cuban revolution was held in Santiago de Cuba, birthplace of Cuban *son* and Afro-Cuban *comparsas* or conga groups, that later gave rise to salsa. The city is home to descendants of slaves, and to Haitian immigrants; Fidel Castro proclaimed the victory of the revolution there on January 1, 1959. We danced, snaking through the city throughout the night to the sound of drums, horns, wood batons, and guitars.

At the conclusion of the conference Castro himself passionately proclaimed that "this continent is pregnant with revolution." He coupled this declaration with a frontal attack on the socialist countries: "If internationalism exists, if solidarity is a word worthy of being uttered, the least that we can expect from any state in the socialist camp [understood to mean the Soviet Union] is to deny financial or technical aid to any of these governments . . . [that] aid imperialism in its attempt to starve the Cuban people to death."[2]

A few nights later, in the wee hours of the morning, Josie and I stood next to Castro with a small group of Chilean socialists from Salvador Allende's political party as they demanded the comandante's advice on how to move forward to power in their country. "*¡Compañeros!*" he replied. "*¡Hay que hacer la revolución!*" ("Comrades! You have to make revolution!") Then he repeated it, slowly, twice, giving emphasis to each word: "*¡Hay que hacer la revolución! ¡Hay que hacer la revolución!*" While his brief answer was little more than a rhetorical gesture, the Chileans seemed delighted.

Seated next to Castro on the OLAS stage was Stokely Carmichael, a leader of the Student Non-violent Coordinating Committee and the conference's guest of honor. I attended, with some 150 media reps from around the world, Stokely's mind-boggling press conference at the Habana Libre hotel. All in white, wearing dark glasses—a sartorial masterpiece—the tall, handsome, eloquent advocate of Black Power stood alongside fellow SNCC members George Ware and Julius Lester, sparking the crowd to applause, laughter and cheers. "Because our color has been used as a weapon to oppress us, we must use our color as a weapon of liberation," he declaimed. I headed my article to Algiers that night with his statement that three major revolutions in the world had been led by "Black men: Mao Zedong, Ho Chi Minh, and Mahatma Gandhi."

That press conference took place in a world undergoing violent transformation. The United States was deep into the war in Vietnam. The Black population of Detroit had launched the largest revolt in US history, tearing the city apart. Che Guevara was fighting in Bolivia, and guerrillas were on the loose in Venezuela, Guatemala, and Nicaragua. Stokely described the white man's world as moribund. He predicted its demise.

After the press conference, I stepped up and introduced myself. "Will the world tour you announced include Africa?" I asked. He said he was leaving for Vietnam and would be delighted to stop in Algeria on his return. Mustapha Bouarfa, head of the Algerian delegation, agreed. The three of us met and Bouarfa issued a formal invitation on behalf of the FLN.

Carmichael arrived in Algiers on September 6, 1967. As his interpreter, I was on hand at the airport and attended his meetings with officials and journalists. His first words as he descended the stairs to the tarmac: "Here I am, finally, in the mother country."

Stokely and I traveled together around the country. He was received by local authorities, as well as student and community groups. He talked about racism at all our appearances, which were reported in the press every day. On a large estate near Oran, self-managed by the former employees of a French settler, we were treated to a fabulous *mechoui*, whole lambs roasted on spits, seasoned with fresh herbs and accompanied by platters of *mesfouf*, a delicious sugared couscous. We sat at long tables and Stokely addressed the crowd with a mixture of charm and militancy. He placed the accent on Black Power as an integral element in the struggle against imperialism. We were surely the first Americans the workers on that estate had ever seen. They applauded him roundly and offered us baskets of fruit.

Cherif Belkacem, head of the FLN, the sole authorized political party in the country, promised offices, residency and support should he decide to set up in Algeria. I believe Stokely was pleased with the welcome he received, although he was not the sort to show emotion, unless it was calculated to drive home a political statement. He and I did not develop any sort of complicity, although he said in his memoirs that I was "very nice."

While in Algiers, Stokely contacted the Guinean embassy and made arrangements to leave for Conakry, a trip that changed the course of his life.

He was received there by President Ahmed Sékou Touré and his prominent permanent guest, Kwame Nkrumah, former president of Ghana, ousted by a coup d'état in 1966, a year after Ben Bella. Nkrumah became Stokely's mentor until his death. Sékou Touré also introduced him to Miriam Makeba, the internationally known South African chanteuse.

Stokely had warned me that he would be followed to Algiers by his friend Kathi Simms, a petite, very pretty African American from Philadelphia. He asked me to look after her and put her on a plane to Conakry, which I did. To my surprise, Kathi turned up in Algiers unannounced and alone a few weeks later. Stokely had fallen in love with Miriam; they would soon marry.

Kathi stayed with me for several weeks, during which time we cut and sewed a large red poncho to help her weather the chill of the northern hemisphere's winter. How she would weather the brutal collapse of her love affair with Stokely seemed more difficult. "You'll forget him," I told her, though I wasn't so sure. She was a wonderfully intelligent, warm companion and I was sorry to see her leave Algiers.

In late 1968, my friend Mohamed Benyahia, then minister of information, asked me to join the staff he was assembling to organize the first Pan-African Cultural Festival, scheduled for July 1969 under the auspices of the Organization of African Unity.

I was the only American in the Algerian administration during those years.

In June 1969, my life took a dramatic spin that catapulted me into contact with the Black Panther Party, an encounter that would reunite me with the country I had left behind so many years before.

At the time, the BPP was the most notorious and noteworthy militant Black organization in the United States. For FBI director, J. Edgar Hoover, the Panthers were "the greatest threat to the internal security of the country." On August 25, 1967, in a memorandum addressed to his twenty-three field offices, he provided new muscle to a counterinsurgency operation called COINTELPRO, directing them "to expose, disrupt, misdirect, discredit or otherwise neutralize the activities of black nationalists." He ordered them "to destroy what the BPP stands for."[3]

Presidents Lyndon Johnson and Richard Nixon both saw a foreign hand in the opposition to the Vietnam War and gradually involved the CIA in spying on American citizens living and traveling abroad, in direct contravention of the agency's mandate from Congress. Soon to be included among the 300,000 Americans on whom the ultra-secret unit, MH/CHAOS, operating from the basement of CIA headquarters, began collecting information were the Black Panthers who would travel to Algiers—and me.[4]

The BPP was known as much for its look as for its actions and politics. Panther militants dressed in black leather from head to toe, wore Afros, and paraded with loaded guns held prominently aloft. Their rhetoric resonated with all of us: "Power to the people" and "Off the pigs" became everyday expressions. Their actions could be benign—breakfast for children, health care, after-school programs—or hard-hitting. They called themselves the vanguard of the revolution, the American Revolution. Their impact was tremendous and would be long lasting.

In my years abroad, I had continued to follow events in the United States and lived vicariously the demonstrations against the war in Vietnam. The upsurge of Black and minority revolt— riots, demonstrations, underground activities—had been high on my agenda for years. I had written about them extensively at the APS and the RTA. As a result my encounter with the Panthers was not simply a chance meeting or a blind date. I knew who they were, and had followed their activities since their startling beginnings. Huey Newton, Bobby Seale, and Eldridge Cleaver were familiar names to me; I was blown away by their audacity and political savvy.

Late one night in early June 1969, as I stepped off the elevator in my building, I heard the phone ringing and rushed up the half-flight of stairs to my apartment. It was Charles Chikerema, representative in Algiers of the Zimbabwe African People's Union, the militant liberation movement of Southern Rhodesia, a country ruled at that time by a minority government of rabidly racist white settlers. Charles said he had been calling for hours. His message was brief: "Eldridge Cleaver is in town and needs help."

No explanation. He gave me the address of the Victoria Hotel. "Go see him!"

Eldridge Cleaver

Eldridge Cleaver was the author of *Soul on Ice*, the astounding book of wisdom and confession that had turned him into a celebrity. He was minister of information of the Black Panther Party, its indefatigable organizer and orator, and creator of the Free Huey campaign (Huey Newton, the party's leader, was in prison awaiting trial for murder). Under his leadership, the Black Panther Party had mushroomed to more than forty chapters and had developed a paramilitary underground network. He also edited the Black Panther newspaper that boasted a circulation of some 200,000 copies.

In April 1968, following Martin Luther King's assassination, Cleaver was caught up in a shootout with the police in Oakland, California. He was wounded, while fellow Panther Bobby Hutton was killed. Three police officers were also wounded, and Cleaver was charged with attempted murder. Awaiting trial, he was released from prison on a writ of habeas corpus. He then ran for president of the United States on the Peace and Freedom Party list, crisscrossing the country speaking to excited crowds. In November 1968, he was accused of parole violation and ordered back to prison; but the Supreme Court of California deemed him a "model parolee," whose return to prison stemmed from "his undue eloquence in pursuing political goals which were offensive to many of his contemporaries." The court was overruled on appeal.

Cleaver knew the system: "I had been State-raised. I climbed the ladder from Juvenile Hall in Los Angeles, starting at the age of twelve, to Folsom Prison, making all the stops in between."[5] And the system knew him: he feared that a return to prison might lead to his death. In any event, Huey Newton's order that he leave the country made his departure final.

A group of his supporters made contact with Cuban emissaries at the UN. According to Cleaver's account in his autobiography, *Soul on Fire*, he was made up as an old man, with a baggy suit and shuffling gait, when he boarded a plane to Montreal. Other versions of his escape have him disguised as an international traveler, the consummate diplomat: dark suit, bowler hat, and pencil mustache. He left Canada hidden on a cargo boat bound for Cuba, arriving on Christmas Eve, 1968.

Early on the morning after Charles's phone call, I walked down a short side street located between the Casbah and the "European" section of the city to the Victoria Hotel. It was drizzling, as I remember. An attendant, wedged in behind a narrow counter at the end of a short entrance hallway, gave me the room number. I mounted the steps to the fourth floor with some trepidation. I was curious and anxious. What could this forty-year-old white woman do for a leader of the Black Panthers in Algiers?

I knocked. Cleaver opened the door. He was twice my size, a powerhouse of a man whose body outdid the small room. I could see the top of his head swipe the ceiling, then dip a bit. His wife Kathleen, heavily pregnant, was stretched out on one of two beds. She nodded to me.

We remained standing and Cleaver talked. As he spoke, the upper half of his body effected a slight lateral movement, though he looked me straight in the eyes. He had impressive hands, with the longest, straightest fingers I had ever seen. He used them to illustrate and underscore, and to smoke. We both smoked, despite the pregnant woman on the bed. The room became hazy.

Cleaver told me that day how he had run afoul of the authorities in Cuba by trying to reunite with other African-American asylum seekers, most of whom were hijackers with warrants out for their arrest in the United States. Contrary to their expectations, the exiles were not received with open arms as fellow revolutionaries: instead they were subjected to intense interrogation and, in most cases, isolation. Many were living and working on farm camps in the Cuban countryside; others had been put in prison.

These were delicate issues for the Cuban authorities, whose support for American activists had become more circumspect over time. For whatever reasons, they had decided that Cleaver should be content to remain a clandestine guest in Cuba. He had expected more: to be hailed and supported as the head of a liberation movement, with privileges like a radio program transmitting to the US, and guerrilla training for BPP militants. He was aware of the enthusiastic welcomes Robert Williams and Stokely Carmichael had received. Stokely had traveled with Castro, he'd sat next to him on stage in Havana. Cleaver never even met the Cuban leader.

Cleaver pursued his agenda nonetheless, and gradually filled his apartment with wanted Americans. When—five months into his stay—Reuters disclosed his presence in the Cuban capital, he was deemed too heavy a burden by his hosts. The informant had been an American woman: Bunny Hearne, an admirer of the Cuban revolution who knew most of the Cuban elite, including Fidel.[6]

"The Cubans dumped me," Cleaver told me. They convinced him that he would be welcomed in Algeria, able to engage more freely in political activity there than in Cuba. All arrangements, they said, had been made, including Cuban travel documents. But on arrival at the airport in Algiers, there had been no reception committee—only a Cuban embassy official. Then, Cleaver's contact at the Cuban embassy reported that the Algerian authorities no longer agreed to harbor him. As a result, the Cubans were proposing to send him on to Jordan or Syria, with his final destination one of the Palestinian liberation movement's camps in those countries. They had ticketed him for departure on the next plane to the Middle East.

Cleaver interrupted his tale, picked up some plane tickets lying on the dresser and waved them in the air: "Can you help me?" he said.

Something was amiss. I was remembering the warm welcome and offers of political status that Stokely Carmichael had received in Algeria two years earlier, and how ready the authorities had always been to help other Americans who came through, even the unaffiliated stragglers. I couldn't count the number of times I had been asked to come down to the FLN headquarters to meet some Americans, usually Blacks, who had arrived on the door-step with no understanding of where they were or how they would survive in a country in which they had no contacts, and spoke neither French nor Arabic. The party functionaries had always acted with kindness, often supplying temporary housing and a few dinars.

Had the Cubans really laid out their plan and received a negative reply? It was hard to believe. "Curious," I said, "it's not in the nature of things here. I know the man in charge of liberation organizations. I'll call him."

Eldridge left the room, went across the hall, and brought back Bob Scheer. Scheer, a well-known radical journalist, editor of *Ramparts* magazine and a member of Fair Play for Cuba, was a close friend and advisor to Cleaver; he had trailed him immediately to Algiers. By the time Scheer entered the room, I had pushed aside a pile of clothes on the second bed and sat down. I was more at ease by then: I knew what had to be done.

A few hours later I was able to speak to commandant Slimane Hoffman, head of the FLN's office in charge of liberation movements. The conversation was brief. I explained who Cleaver was, just in case: after all, Algiers is a long way from Oakland, California. I explained that he had arrived in Algiers from Cuba, and that he hoped to stay in the country and announce his arrival with an international press conference. Apprehensive, I took a deep breath and waited for him to respond.

Hoffman had an interesting, unique background for an Algerian political cadre. His father was a member of the French Foreign Legion; his mother was Algerian. He had been a professional soldier in the French Army, a tank specialist. In 1957, with a small group of Algerian comrades, all officers, he had deserted to join the Algerian Liberation Army. He would later be named "wali of the Algiers Wilaya," that is, governor of the capital and its region.

"No problem," was Hoffman's laconic reply. He had one condition: that the announcement of Cleaver's presence in Algiers be made first by APS.

How the Cuban embassy took this news I never knew. Bob Scheer said I had "pulled their chestnuts out of the fire," and told them so. I did learn that the Algerians had never been informed of the arrangements for Cleaver's transfer. They were, however, aware of Kathleen's arrival, and had wondered why she was holed up in a nondescript hotel near the harbor with a Cuban, or at any rate a man carrying Cuban travel documents.

Eldridge was convinced he had been "double-crossed"; but why? Was it because relations between the Castro regime and Boumediene's Algeria had soured so mightily since the coup d'état that cooperation between the two countries was at a virtual standstill? Or was Eldridge's fate the fault of incompetent and incoherent Cuban emissaries in Algiers, isolated and out of touch with the authorities? Whatever the case, he was uneasy with the game the Cubans were playing and wondered out loud whether they intended to "off" him.

Afterward, he said: "You saved my life."

"Come on, Eldridge, all I did was make a phone call."

The group in Algiers—Bob Scheer, Kathleen, and Eldridge—had been cloistered inside their hotel, dependent on the Cuban embassy's car. I had "wheels," as Eldridge labeled my Mini, and was able to take them on a tour. I introduced them to La Pêcherie, an open-air fish restaurant below the Casbah facing the sea. Technically speaking, they were undercover until Eldridge surfaced officially, but Scheer and Cleaver from then on displayed themselves regularly at La Pêcherie. They stood out like camels at a ski resort, but the news of their presence somehow remained closeted until the press conference.

Scheer and Cleaver saw to the details with precision. Reuters was brought in at the planning stage. It was difficult keeping them at bay. I had to keep reminding them of Hoffman's condition that the first press release be made through the Algerian press agency. The announcement hit the Reuters wire a few minutes after the official APS communiqué.

The press conference took place on July 15 at the University of Algiers, in the Salle des Actes, in the center of the city. The auditorium was filled with Algerian and foreign journalists, students, liberation movement representatives, and diplomatic personnel. This was Cleaver's first public appearance since the day he had vanished from San Francisco in November 1968.

Eldridge was taut, nervous—he couldn't stop pacing. He had Kathleen dig through their luggage for a favorite brightly colored dashiki and a gold ear hoop. Whatever her state of pregnancy, she looked amazing: her impeccable hairdo—the Afro she had displayed all across the United States—plus dark glasses.

Kathleen, Eldridge and I sat on the dais. In a low voice I repeated in English what was being said in French on the floor. Julia Wright (Ellen and Richard Wright's daughter) and her husband, Henri Hervé, had come over from Paris to interpret from English into French for the audience.

Hervé, used to a Parisian university climate where roughly addressing students with orders to "shut up," "sit down," "get out," etc. was de rigueur, misjudged the crowd. His brusque interjections of "*assieds-toi*" and "*ta gueule*," as the meeting got rolling and people tried to intervene, were met with cries of anger. He was hissed off the stage. No one in postcolonial Algeria was going to accept being bullied by a Frenchman. Julia took over interpreting.

Eldridge spoke about the struggle in the US, about his excitement to be in Algiers, to be in Africa. "We are an integral part of Africa's history. White America teaches us that our history begins on the plantations, that we have no other past. We have to take back our culture."

"Oppressed people need unity based on revolutionary principles rather than skin color," he said, adding: "Our goal is to break the system." He closed with, "Our struggle is revolutionary."

The Pan-African Cultural Festival

The Pan-African Cultural Festival was scheduled to take place in Algiers from July 21 to August 1, 1969. Every country on the continent of Africa, as well as the African diaspora, was sending artists, musicians, and intellectuals to take part in an explosive outdoor extravaganza. Also on the agenda were symposia and conferences on cultural and economic themes. One of my tasks had been to contribute to a list of African Americans to be invited, so the Black Panther Party had been keyed in well before Eldridge Cleaver arrived in Algiers. I immediately informed my boss, Mohamed Benyahia, of the arrival of Cleaver and his group.

In the week before the festival, all the hotels and government villas were emptied of their occupants so as to house participants. Arrangements were made for the Panther group to move into the Hotel Aletti, the art deco hotel in the center of town inaugurated by Charlie Chaplin in 1930. The BPP was also provided with a storefront locale on rue Didouche Mourad, one of the two main thoroughfares of the city, to use as their base. Their Afro-American Center became one of the festival's focal points, with information sessions, discussions and films all day long and well into the night. Chief of Staff David Hilliard, Minister of Education Raymond (Masai) Hewitt, and Minister of Culture Emory Douglas had arrived from the States with Panther newspapers and pamphlets which they passed out liberally to the young Algerians who crowded the Center, intrigued with Panther ideology and fascinated by their personas and their grace.

Four thousand participants paraded through the streets of Algiers on the opening day. They represented twenty-four countries and the diaspora in others, including the United States. Musicians and dancers performed along rue Didouche Mourad and rue Larbi Ben M'hidi to the sounds of African drums and horns. Veiled women and excited young people cheered, clapped, and *youyou*ed; many pushed into the street and joined the march. Algiers had never seen anything comparable.

All the Americans were sought-after stars of the Pan-Af: musicians Archie Shepp, Grachan Moncur III, Sunny Murray, Cal Massey, Clifford Thornton, Alan Silva, Dave Burrell, and Oscar Peterson; singers Nina Simone and Marion Williams; poets Maya Angelou, Don Lee, and Ted Joans; writers Ed Bullins, Barbara Chase-Riboud, Nathan Hare, and Julia Wright. Plus Stokely Carmichael, back in Algiers with his wife Miriam Makeba.

I was on hand in the lobby of the Hotel Aletti to witness the first encounter between Cleaver and Archie Shepp, the great jazz saxophonist. They eyed one another in recognition, skirted each other, and then their hands met in complicated symmetry and their bodies swayed before a word was spoken. What they said was banal; what the meeting meant was mutual appreciation as African Americans and as revolutionaries, each in his own right.

William Klein, the photographer and filmmaker who had been engaged to produce a documentary of the festival, made an hour-long film about Eldridge and the African-American struggle, paid for by the Algerian government. During the planning stage of the festival, I had been part of a small gathering at Benyahia's home where the merits of the two candidates to direct the festival film were discussed: Marcel Camus and William Klein. Camus had won the Palme d'Or at Cannes in 1959 for his film *Orfeu Negro*, made during the Carnival in Rio. Klein's *Who Are You, Polly Maggoo?* and *The Greatest*, about Muhammad Ali, had also won international acclaim. The latter film tipped the scale in favor of Klein, much to everyone's later regret—filming the Pan-Af had been beyond Klein's organizational skills. The film, despite the extraordinary documents it was based on, was an indigestible flop.

During the festival Cleaver also met with Stokely Carmichael, and the press amply commented upon their verbal battle. Carmichael had resigned from the Black Panther Party and, in an open letter, attacked both its methods and its policy of collaboration with whites. Eldridge slashed back in his particular firebrand style in an open letter: "Your vision was blind. You were unable to distinguish your friends from your enemies because all you could see was the color of the cat's skin."

Meanwhile, Miriam Makeba and I were engaged in getting Nina Simone on stage. Raging drunk, she had barricaded herself in her room at the Hôtel Saint-Georges. At the top of her voice, she upbraided us: "I don't have any friends. Get the fuck outta here!" We canceled the first of her four scheduled performances. The next morning, at rehearsal, she shocked the Algerian stagehands; they had never seen a woman drunk. For the evening's performance, Miriam and I managed to drag her on stage where she resembled a pinpricked balloon slowly sagging. For the last two shows she managed well, decked out in a tightly wound conical white turban and a long, wide-striped gown that flared at the bottom, her shoulders bare. She enthralled the crowd—which included President Boumediene—with her version of Jacques Brel's "*Ne me quitte pas.*"

Shepp and the musicians provided a climactic finish to the festival, an unexpected symbolic "happening." They appeared with a large group of Touareg percussionists and dancers wearing flowing white robes and intricate white turbans. The Americans, dressed in everyday casual attire, improvised, fitting jazz to traditional Saharan music. It was magic: a dramatic moment, a bolt of lightning for everyone there. Yes, indeed, as Archie proclaimed loud and strong: "We are still Black and we have come back . . . Jazz is a Black Power! Jazz is an African power! *Nous sommes revenus!*"

That performance made a deep impression on the Algerians in the theater, including Benyahia, who was a jazz lover. In the New York years of the UN debates on Algeria, he and I would spend hours in Sam Goody's buying records for him to take back to Tunis. The result was an invitation to the desert south, where an Algerian crew organized and filmed another performance by Archie and his musicians in the Touaregs' home environment. "I haven't played so well for a long time," Archie said, after experimenting with local instruments like the *karkabous* (metal or wood castanets) and the *ghayta* (a reed instrument similar to an oboe). On his return to Algiers, he confided to me, "I have just lived one of the most profound experiences of my life."

On the last night the people of Algiers joined the delegations marching and performing through the streets and on the squares of the city, in an awesome interplay of delight and understanding. The Algerian capital was bathed in light; the fireworks that burst and shimmered over the waters of the Mediterranean and on the city constituted the most extravagant display of pyrotechnics ever seen in Africa.

Capital of the Third World

The Algerian war for independence had lasted close to eight years, ending officially on July 5, 1962. Algerians, from the bureaucrat to the homemaker, the *fellah*, the schoolchild, were acutely aware of the support received from abroad throughout the war. The local and international press had followed the yearly UN debates closely. Everyone knew the names of their representatives and which countries in the Middle East, the developing world, or the Communist bloc had supported their battle against France. They knew that John F. Kennedy, while a US senator, had directed a scathing attack against France for waging a colonial war. They knew that the ALN had trained freedom fighters from other countries during their own struggle.

Once independence was achieved, no one forgot. Algeria adopted an open-door policy of aid to the oppressed, an invitation to liberation and opposition movements and personalities from around the world. All were welcomed: the National Liberation Front of South Vietnam; the Palestinian liberation organizations; exiled politicians from Brazil, Argentina, Spain, Portugal, even neighboring Tunisia and Morocco; representatives of liberation movements in South Africa, Ethiopia, Southwest Africa, Angola, Mozambique, Guinea Bissau, and Canada, with the Front de Libération du Québec; and those fighting guerrilla wars in Venezuela, Guatemala, and Nicaragua.

The reception the Black Panther Party received in Algiers was in line with the country's foreign policy at the time. It has been said that recognition of the Black Panthers was only possible because no diplomatic relations had existed between the United States and Algeria since the 1967 Arab–Israeli war. I feel certain that Algeria's treatment of the Panthers flowed naturally from its position as a Third World leader, and would not have differed had relations with the United States been reestablished.

Even before he surfaced officially, Eldridge met with Trần Hoài Nam, representative of the Vietcong. The meeting took place just as the American war against Vietnam was at a turning point: the Vietcong's Tet offensive of early 1968 had shaken the

American military and political establishment to the core. Inflamed agitation and protests at home were dogging American complacency. As a result, Lyndon Johnson had refrained from running for reelection. Since January, Richard Nixon had been occupying the White House.

Nam was a small man, slight in build, with a gentle face that belied his staunch convictions, abrasive militancy, and courage. He had great capacity for friendship, and was one of the rare foreign representatives in Algiers who developed close relationships with Algerian leaders. My own relationship with him was warm. He looked on me as the typical American, which amused me. He was anxious for my comments on events in the States; he wanted his associates in Algiers to know me and see how I lived. On Nam's suggestion, I invited his two aides to my apartment for "American" meals.

Nam and I worked together on several projects, including putting together an "Americans for Vietnam" group with the few compatriots living in Algiers or those passing through. Green, a Black jazz pianist, was the spokesman for the group. We made a small splash in the press when a journalist from *Newsweek* called for an interview after seeing the communiqué I sent out over the APS wire. Nam spoke fluent French; I did the interpreting for him and Eldridge. When he was next received by President Boumediene, Nam spoke favorably of the Black Panthers.

The North Korean embassy contacted me to set up a meeting with Cleaver at its Algiers residence. There, the ambassador extended an invitation to the Black Panthers to attend an international conference of journalists (billed as the "International Conference on the Tasks of Journalists of the Whole World in Their Fight Against the Aggression of US Imperialism"), to be held that September in Pyongyang.

We were also guests at the Chinese embassy for a film showing and reception, and exchanged comments with the Chinese ambassador. "China is the friend of the American people," he stated. "Our quarrel is with the American government and their policies." I interjected: "The American government was elected by the American people." My feeling was that you get the government you merit.

These were Cleaver's first encounters with high-level foreign emissaries. He handled himself like a veteran. He was cool, reflective, intelligent, the representative of an indigenous liberation movement establishing relations with countries and movements whose goals were shared to varying degrees. Taking into account what I knew of his past—school dropout, drug dealer, rapist, ex-convict—his capacity to learn and adapt was awesome, and right on time.

As for me, it was thrilling to be involved in American politics again. My old roots were still alive, and I was ready to battle. I don't know how the Panthers saw me, this strange white woman in Algiers, but they were certainly relieved to find someone who could speak the language and knew the conduits of power in this curious country. After all my years of adapting, first to France and then to Algeria, they made me conscious of my American self. I had not discarded it.

Settling In

The festival closed, the delegates left for home, and the Cleavers, whose son Maceo had been born in a Cuban-run hospital in inland Tissemsilt, in the midst of the festival bustle, set about finding living quarters. Algiers had a monstrous housing problem. Despite the departure of the French settler population, people had been pouring into the city from the countryside and occupying anything resembling a housing unit. There had been practically no new construction in the seven years since independence. An old friend, Ali Habib, came to the rescue with an empty house by the sea at Pointe Pescade, a few miles out of the city. It was a godsend, as other comrades were fast arriving, refugees from Cuba: former hijackers Byron Booth and Clinton (Rahim) Smith, James (Akili) Patterson, his wife Gwen, and their daughter Tanya.

The liberation movement representatives sought the Panthers out and close relationships followed, especially with those countries where English was the working language, such as Namibia, Zimbabwe, and South Africa, but also with the Portuguese colonies: Angola, Guinea-Bissau, Mozambique. Eldridge's appearance alongside Fatah's representative in Algiers during the Cultural Festival was picked up by the international press, with the *New York Times* quoting him: "We recognize the Jewish people have suffered, but this suffering should not be used to justify suffering by Arabs now."[7]

Contact with BPP headquarters in California was daily. Visiting delegations of Panther supporters began arriving in Algiers. Journalists seeking exclusive interviews also came to town; they ignored the country in which they found themselves and made a beeline for Eldridge. I remember in particular Lee Lockwood, a freelance photojournalist and authority on Cuba, who would publish a book on his conversations with Cleaver, and Don Schanche, doing in-depth interviews, also for a book on Cleaver. I was witness to Mike Wallace's interview for "60 Minutes" in the house at Pointe Pescade. Eldridge, drunk on rhetoric, projected "taking off the head of Richard Nixon . . . J.

Edgar Hoover, Senator John McClellan, et al . . . They are criminals," he said, "programming oppression and destruction not only in the United States but around the world." A few days after that interview was broadcast on American TV, Wallace's film takes, notes, and even his expense account were subpoenaed by the Justice Department.

Eldridge's royalties from the sales of *Soul on Ice* had been blocked in the US, placed in an escrow account to which he had no access. When it was discovered that he was living in Cuba, the US government accused him of "trading with the enemy." During the Pan-African Festival, David Brodsky, a San Francisco lawyer, arrived with papers to liberate Eldridge from the Trading with the Enemy Act, but he had to appear before a US consular official in order to sign the documents. The two men took off for the US Interests Section of the Swiss Embassy—actually the American Embassy flying a Swiss flag—where Eldridge's signature became official.

I later prepared letters instructing his foreign publishers to transfer royalties to him directly. When he told me that his former lawyer and fiancée Beverly Axelrod received 25 percent of those royalties, I tried to convince him to change his contract with her. "That's a lot of money. You'll need it here." He would not hear of it.

Ellen Wright, who was Richard Wright's widow and a literary agent in Paris, came to Algiers to advance Eldridge money that was later repaid by his literary agent Cyrilly Abels. Funds were also forthcoming from the BPP, Panther support committees in Europe, and many well-wishers.

Working with the Panthers

I was in contact with Eldridge almost daily—through telephone calls, appointments, and visits. He often borrowed my car. When I was away I left him the keys to the Austin and to my apartment. For him, I was neutral. He had no fear: I didn't talk back, and I had no Panther role or history, no claims on the past or the future. There was no sexual connection between us, and he made it clear to everyone in his establishment that I was "out of bounds" for them, too. Eldridge issued that pronouncement as soon as other Panthers began to arrive, and told me he had done so. How right he was. Any liaison with one of his companions would have destroyed the unstated pact that he and I had initiated. Very early on, I realized also that sex between him and me would lead to my own destruction. As events unfolded, I verified how farsighted I had been.

Most important for Eldridge was that I spoke and wrote French. I was his key to the local establishment. Algerians have a tradition of secrecy, they are closed-mouthed: habits that were a necessity during their war against the colonial power have remained entrenched until today. Even foreigners who had been engaged in the struggle became adept at this reticence, myself included. But I was able to explain and interpret events to Eldridge in his new country of residence. I knew people at the top, whom to contact, and could get appointments. Plus, my job at the Ministry of Information left me free to accompany him wherever, whenever. I could always make up my time.

Soon after the Pan-African Cultural Festival ended, Eldridge, accompanied by Byron Booth, who was presented as the deputy field marshal of the BPP, left for Pyongyang and the international journalists' conference.

The two Panthers were the only American delegates. Eldridge addressed the meeting and was elected a member of the conference bureau. He and Byron remained in North Korea for more than a month; they traveled around the country, even stopping at Panmunjom where, according to the press, he challenged a Black American soldier on duty. He met Kim Il-sung twice. On his return to Algiers he told me how impressed he had been by the Korean policy toward children: how happy the little ones were, how well-cared for and loved. He had brought back photos of them and a film to show me. He was anxious to maintain and develop relations, and hoped to take an all-American delegation representing a panoply of organizations to Korea. He also looked forward to various forms of aid.

Not long after his return, early one morning in November, Eldridge turned up in my office at the Ministry of Information. It was a large room with desks lining the walls and facing inward, so that my colleagues and I were all in sight of each other. Zohra Sellami, Behja Bensalem, Mahmoud Tlemsani, and I were working on a mock-up for a slick international news magazine we were to edit for the Ministry. All our friends and contacts knew where to find us and would drop in unannounced. In those days there were no guards, no special security at the entrance to the building. There were always people wandering in and out. My colleagues all knew Eldridge and were duly impressed by him.

This particular day he drew up a chair, sat down at the side of my desk, lowered his eyelids, and murmured: "I have something to tell you. Something happened last night. I killed Rahim."

"What? Oh, my God! What are you saying? Why?"

"He stole all our money, stashed it, and was planning to split."

My head began to swim. The image of Rahim (Clinton Smith) with his big Afro and his slim body flashed through my head. In that tight space I couldn't scream. I couldn't jump up and run. I just sat there and slumped, horrified.

"Byron was there. The two of us took the body up into the hills behind Pointe Pescade and buried him."

All this in whispers. Then he got up, put on his shades, and left me with his bundle of *merde*. His delivery had been clear, direct, with no hint of a conscience disturbed.

Byron and Rahim had escaped from prison in the US and hijacked a plane to Cuba, joining Eldridge in exile. With the help of the Cubans, they had made their way to Algiers. The next time I heard from Eldridge, it was to say that Byron had headed out to somewhere in sub-Saharan Africa.

I was still digesting Eldridge's confession when my friend Daniel told me he had seen Rahim and Kathleen Cleaver very much together at a nightclub, dancing cheek to cheek and "smooching," while Eldridge was in Pyongyang. In less than a week, the corpse—buried crudely and partially uncovered—was found and reported to the police. From the Afro and the tattoos on the body it was deduced that the victim was African American. A French friend of the Panthers, Jean-Marie Boeglin, was called in and identified the body.

Following the February 1971 split in the Black Panther Party, an article appeared in *The Black Panther* stating that Cleaver had killed a fellow Panther in Algiers because he had had an affair with Cleaver's wife. The article, signed by Elaine Brown, named the victim and made absurd charges against President Boumediene and Yasser Arafat, then chairman of the Palestinian Liberation Organization, accusing the first of "endorsing the crime" and providing "the plot of ground in which to bury him," and the second of "accepting" it.

In 2001, Byron Booth was arrested in Nigeria, where he had been living since leaving Algiers, and was extradited to the

United States. According to statements documented in court in California, Booth confirmed his presence at the murder scene. Don "DC" Cox, field marshal of the Black Panther Party, has described the confrontation that he and other members of the Algiers Panthers initiated with Cleaver sometime in 1970. Cleaver's first reaction had been denial but, pressed by the group, he admitted to the killing. According to DC, the weapon, an AK-47, was a gift from Kim Il-sung.

It took me some time to get used to being party to Cleaver's crime. I have often asked myself what I could have done. Turned him in? To whom? The Algerian police, the American embassy? No way.

As far as I know, the police went no further with their investigation and never summoned the Panthers for questioning. Why they decided to let the matter rest is down to conjecture, but they certainly registered the event. Why Eldridge felt he had to burden me with his package of misery is also a matter of conjecture. I can't imagine what I could have done to help him had the Algerian authorities decided to pounce. We never spoke of it again, nor have I ever had a conversation with anyone else on the subject. As for Kathleen, she has blotted it out.

On October 26, 1969, Eldridge addressed a petition to the Algerian government requesting official status as a liberation movement for the International Section of the Black Panther Party. There was no reaction from the authorities; the Panthers interpreted their silence as a no. I was used to bureaucratic inefficiency, the lack of follow-up, the tendency to let matters ride, and was not as certain as they. Add to that list the reluctance of the authorities to put anything in writing. The Panthers were firmly installed in Algiers; no one questioned their presence. For me, that was the equivalent of saying yes, you're official.

Other Panthers came: in May 1970, Don Cox arrived. In late June, Sekou Odinga and Larry Mack (of the New York 21),[8] through Cuba, their transit point to Algiers. In July, Pete O'Neal, head of the Panther branch in Kansas City, and his wife Charlotte, who gave birth to their first child in Algeria.

The International Section intensified contacts with other liberation movements, even initiating secret training sessions in the use of arms for the Ethiopian and the South African contingents present in Algiers. Panthers became the unofficial bodyguards of Oliver Tambo, Nelson Mandela's former law partner and head of the African National Congress of South Africa, during his frequent visits. Don Cox traveled with Tambo, "offering my body as a shield."

"Wheels" were a constant headache. None of the Panthers' housing was in the city center, and local bus services were complicated and inadequate. Two rented French cars served their purposes for a while; the FLN occasionally helped out with a chauffeur-driven vehicle. The problem was eventually resolved by German supporters offering a slightly used beige Volkswagen van.

There was an aura of glamor surrounding the Panthers. They were the admired stars of the local scene, but in the atmosphere of that closed society their flamboyance was also looked upon critically. Their lifestyle was American: they were generous, outspoken, and free. They provided themselves with advantages—for them, necessities—that other liberation movements would never obtain: houses, cars, media coverage, visiting celebrities. They dated and could be seen around town with attractive women, both Algerian and foreign. I can still picture Sekou

Odinga next to a lovely auburn-haired American, swooping down rue Didouche Mourad in a shiny red convertible with the top down and her at the wheel. They were highly visible guests in a shaded, conservative environment.

One morning in the late spring of 1970, Eldridge called and invited me to lunch in a downtown restaurant. Before he could tell me what was on his mind, an American we knew vaguely sat down at the next table and tried to engage us in conversation. Eldridge rose from his seat and literally picked the man up by the collar and shooed him out of the restaurant. He had a purpose in mind and was impatient to express it; he brooked no interruption. He wanted to be recognized officially, he wanted a well-equipped office, and he wanted to be able to operate from a single locale—with government aid. I was to come up with a solution to the Panthers' installation problems.

I thought it through and contacted the one person who could make it happen if he so decided: Mhamed Yazid, one of the few Algerians with firsthand knowledge of the United States—his wife, Olive, was American. Yazid and a colleague, Hocine Aït-Ahmed, first landed in New York in the early days of the war, in 1955. Their mission was to gain an entrée to the United Nations in order to defend the Algerian cause in front of that assembly. At the time neither of the men spoke fluent English; they had but a few dollars between them and not a single contact. I heard Yazid tell the story many times, never failing to mention that he, the gourmet and cook, "had subsisted on peanut-butter sandwiches."

Before they returned to North Africa, they had achieved the improbable: they had convinced countries sympathetic to the Algerian cause to provide them with UN accreditation and political input. They had an office and the means to finance it. The

Algerian question was put on the General Assembly agenda every succeeding year. Yazid became the first permanent representative in New York; he attended every annual debate until independence. From 1958 to 1962, he was minister of information of the GPRA. His trips to New York were frequent. I knew him well.

Mhamed's reaction to the problem I presented was to invite a group of us to lunch at his home in Blida, *la ville des roses*, located on the fertile plain on the outskirts of Algiers. He wanted to see the Panthers close up.

The weather was on our side, balmy and warm. A table had been set up in the large enclosed garden of the old family residence, built in the time of the Turks. Eldridge, Kathleen, DC and I were treated to the refined Algerian cooking of Yazid's elderly grandmother. I remember with delight her couscous, steamed and buttered in the traditional way, with fresh lima beans from the garden.

Mhamed was an exceptional storyteller with a good sense of humor. Peppering his English with everyday expressions, street talk, even sayings and proverbs, was an old trick that he had used to advantage countless times with the press at the United Nations. He was canny and a shrewd observer who beguiled his guests with stories of his life in the United States, all the while sizing them up. The outcome of the "interview" was affirmative. Soon afterward, he called to say that the National Liberation Front of South Vietnam was moving to embassy status and vacating its Algerian government villa in El Biar, a neighborhood in the hills above the city. That property would be assigned to the Panthers.

Status as a recognized liberation movement carried with it other advantages: telephone and telex connections, Algerian ID cards as special residents, the possibility to come in and out of the country without entry or exit visas for themselves and their announced guests, and a monthly cash stipend. They joined a list of liberation movements enjoying such privileges, but were one of the rare few with a government villa.

Why the Algerian authorities singled out the BPP for formal recognition and privileged treatment is a legitimate question. They could have let things roll on as they were. Were negotiations with the US for Algerian gas advancing?[9] If so, the International Section could possibly serve as a ploy for one side or the other.

On the other hand, Algeria was very clearly part of the Third World, and its international language and positions definitely aligned with the eastern bloc. The Soviet Union, Bulgaria, Czechoslovakia, and East Germany had furnished aid in armaments, training and education during the liberation war. It was also clear, however, that within the power structure there was a current of opinion anxious to get along better with the US. And Algeria was not Cuba.

The Inauguration

Kathleen was pregnant a second time. At the end of May 1970, Eldridge shipped her and little Maceo off to North Korea, where she was expected to give birth in late August or early September. She was followed shortly afterward by Barbara Easley, DC's companion, who was also pregnant.

Eldridge had just met a gorgeous young Algerian, Malika Ziri, and he was in love. Malika was constantly at his side; he took her everywhere; they could not bear to be apart. I observed with surprise that behind his stoic shell there was tenderness. Everyone was attracted to tall, lithe Malika. She had charm and intelligence. Attaching herself publicly to a Black American at least fifteen years her senior, in a closed society where discretion is the byword, took a good deal of confidence. She was a brave woman.

In the middle of July, Eldridge left Algiers to co-chair, with Bob Scheer, a delegation of eleven Americans, named the American Anti-Imperialist Delegation, traveling to North Korea, then on to North Vietnam and China. Their goal was to express their solidarity and condemn US imperialism. In Hanoi they had an historic meeting with General Võ Nguyên Giáp, the man who had defeated the French and was in the process of defeating the American war machine. In a taped radio broadcast, Eldridge called on Black American soldiers to revolt, to refuse to fight, to desert, to sabotage the war from within.

The Cleavers' daughter, Joju Younghi, was born in Pyongyang on August 31 and received her name from the first lady of Korea, the actress Kim Sung-ae. On her return to Algiers, Kathleen came face to face with Malika and had to endure this new reality in her family life.

During Cleaver's absence, DC, Sekou Odinga, and Larry Mack, along with non-refugees Bill Stephens and Connie Matthews, prepared the large white stucco villa for residence and work. DC drew up, in military style, daily routines and assignments for the cleanup, painting, furnishing and installation. Bronze plaques in Arabic and English, placed at the gated entrance to the villa, announced its occupants as the International Section of the Black Panther Party and sported a panther logo.

With the return of the Anti-Imperialist Delegation to Algiers, the official inauguration took place on September 13, 1970. "This is the first time in the struggle of the Black people in America that they have established representation abroad," said Cleaver. The crowd at what became known as the Embassy included representatives of the diplomatic corps, Algerian officials, representatives of other liberation movements, and the press. Sanche de Gramont (alias Ted Morgan), a prominent French-American journalist in town for the event, published a lead story in the *New York Times Magazine* a few weeks later entitled "Our Other Man in Algiers." It carried photos of Eldridge and me with the counselor of the Chinese embassy, and of the plaque at the gate. The Panthers had arrived.

The "other man" and I visited the other American embassy in Algiers a number of times—that is, the one flying the Swiss flag, since Algeria had abruptly severed diplomatic relations during the 1967 Arab–Israeli war. Our visits were part curiosity and part thrill but also involved, when required, a request for an official document, like a passport for one of the children. On one occasion Eldridge walked out of the compound with the US government seal under his jacket, a heavy metal contraption designed to grip official papers between its paws and imprint them with the American eagle. Once in the car, Eldridge loosened his arms around his jacket and displayed it. I had been right next to him but hadn't seen a thing. The word went out to bring it back, no questions asked, which was done.

We attended a few receptions at the other embassy—on Thanksgiving Day 1970, Eldridge, three other Panthers, and I showed up for the holiday festivities, even shook hands with William Eagleton, chief of the US Interest Section—a euphemism for "ambassador." We had a few cordial encounters with Frank Wisner Jr., a junior diplomat on his first overseas assignment and the son of another Frank Wisner, who in 1947 established and headed the CIA's counterinsurgency department. This was the spy and sabotage wing known as the Office of Policy

Coordination. He is credited with masterminding the overthrow of Mossadegh in Iran and Árbenz in Guatemala. The elder Wisner committed suicide in 1965, with one of his son's guns, it is said. Wisner Jr. presented himself as the "cool dude," capable of understanding the Panthers. Awareness of his father's record made us extremely cautious. Given the fundamental allegiances on either side, the contact was short-lived.

Eldridge rented a comfortable, sunlit villa in Hydra, paying a full year's rent in advance, in dollars. It served as private meeting place, nursery for the half-dozen infants in tow, living quarters for the Cleavers, DC, and Barbara Easley, and occasional hotel for special guests.

5

New Arrivals

Soon after the opening of the Panther embassy, however, disaster struck with the arrival in Algiers, on September 25, 1970, of Timothy and Rosemary Leary. The high priest of LSD had escaped from a US prison thanks to the Weather Underground and a "donation" of $25,000 (some say $50,000) from the Brotherhood of Eternal Love, a California hippy group devoted to the manufacture of LSD and the diffusion of high-grade marijuana. Rosemary had arranged travel documents and tickets; Timothy shimmied over a wall and was whisked away to freedom by the Weathermen.

According to Eldridge, the San Luis Obispo internment center Leary had left behind was a "camp for white internees," not a real prison. Stew Albert of the counterculture Youth International Party, or Yippies, flew in a few days prior to the two exiles with a mission to inform the Panthers of their impending arrival and to facilitate their installation in Algiers. Eldridge and I both felt that Leary was a hot potato that had to be cooled before the news made headlines and the Algerian authorities learned of his presence in the country. Hadn't Richard Nixon declared Leary "the most dangerous man in the United States"?

I fixed up an appointment with Slimane Hoffman, the FLN official in charge of liberation movements. We provided him with a toned-down version of Leary's background, emphasizing his history as a Harvard professor. Eldridge assured Hoffman that he was capable of controlling Leary's drug use and his potential verbal excesses. I think the commandant was amused. He wished us well.

Leary spent his first few days in Algeria in a roundtable free-for-all at the Cleavers' private villa. Eldridge's intention was to convince or coerce this willful, highly articulate ego-tripper to convert to revolution, to discipline himself and denounce hard drugs publicly. This was indeed a tall order. My role was to make sure he understood the country he was now residing in and the dangers his presence posed for the entire Panther operation, as well as himself, if he stepped out of line. I provided a frightening description of the inside of an Algerian jail—even though I had never seen one—in the hope that he would balk at the thought of being locked up. Concretely, Eldridge planned to interview Leary on film for a US audience and have him denounce drugs. He agreed.

The interview was filmed at the Embassy. Eldridge opened the discussion of "the drug culture and the American revolution" by denouncing the idea of liberation through drugs as the invention of "illusionary guys." The road to revolution, he argued, lay with organizations like the Weathermen and the BPP that were involved in direct action. Leary's response was first evasive, then inconclusive, and finally contradictory: "I think it is a mistake for we sitting here in Algeria to be making pronouncements about the United States in a general way beyond one statement, that revolution is ongoing. It is a crucial period. It is no time for escape. If taking any drug postpones for ten minutes the revolution, the liberation of our sisters and brothers, our comrades, then taking drugs must be postponed for ten minutes ...

However, if one hundred FBI agents agreed to take LSD, thirty would certainly drop out." Such was his jubilant conclusion.

Séverine and Ali Aït-Kasimi, a French-Algerian couple I knew who were leaving the country, agreed—for $2,000 in key money—to turn over their attractive two-bedroom apartment, on boulevard Télemly in central Algiers, to the Learys. It was decorated with a mix of modern pieces and handcrafted Algerian furniture. A proud, dark, wooden Berber chest greeted guests as they entered. The Learys overhauled the place so as to resume their own pattern of home life: with rugs, furs, and cushions, they created a laid-back sitting-on-floor environment. They quickly became socially active with local people and with groupies from the US who traipsed across the Atlantic for the love of Tim.

My first impressions of Tim and Rosemary were of aging hipsters, passé stars from the silent film era. I don't know what I had expected: something visually crazier, flamboyant, exciting. Take away the LSD and they became ordinary.

As part of his projected transformation, it was decided that Leary should accompany DC, Marty Kenner, and Jennifer Dohrn (sister of Bernardine Dohrn, the famous Students for a Democratic Society militant and Weatherwoman) to the Middle East, on an invitation from Fatah. Let him surface there, it was decided, not in Algeria.

Their trip was thwarted at every stop. The group landed in Cairo and were welcomed by the Egyptian authorities and taken to a hotel paid for by the Algerian embassy. But there the telephone and cable lines were down, and they were unable to communicate with the International Section back in Algiers. As a result, when they flew into Beirut, there was no one to meet them. The airport authorities directed them to a hotel that turned out to be the headquarters of the Western press. Leary was recognized, and the hotel at once besieged; the group was followed everywhere by crowds of reporters and cameras. It became physically and politically impossible to continue the journey to the Fatah training camps in Jordan and Syria. They returned to Cairo, where Leary, paranoid and hysterical, became "uncontrollable," DC reported. He started jumping over walls, hiding behind buildings, raising his arms and screaming for help in the streets. The group contacted the Algerian ambassador, who arranged for their return by plane to Algiers.

As a contribution to making Leary over as a revolutionary critical of drugs, Mokhtar Maherzi, an astute interviewer and writer, and I undertook an in-depth interview that, strategically placed in English and French publications, would unveil the "new" Tim. We held several successful recording sessions— until one evening at my apartment, when the doorbell rang and four young Americans irrupted into our space. As if at the strike of a match, Leary lit up. He was transformed, exchanging "acid" slogans with his groupies. By the time we picked up the interview again, Leary had become his old egomaniacal self. Posturing in front of his admirers, he enumerated the benefits of "turning on" with LSD. When he went on to claim that heroin, "taken properly," was not addictive, Mokhtar turned off the recorder.

The Learys rented a car and began taking trips to Bou Saâda, an oasis in the Sahara where, lounging on colorful handloom carpets, they partied with LSD. Algeria is an immense country, four-fifths desert but, curiously, it is one of those places in the world where one is never quite alone. At any moment, nomads, fellahin, or shepherds can appear out of nowhere, as they did with the Learys who, in chemistry's grip, would smile broadly and wave to the dumbfounded onlookers.

The Panthers reacted strongly to these escapades and, in February 1971, "arrested" the Learys, putting them under guard for several days. Eldridge filmed the prisoners and issued a press release distributed in the States: "Something's wrong with Leary's brain . . . We want people to gather their wits, sober up and get down to the serious business of destroying the Babylonian empire . . . To all those of you who look to Dr. Leary for inspiration and leadership, we want to say to you that your god is dead because his mind has been blown by acid."

Once "liberated," however, Leary complained to the Algerian authorities, and Hoffman asked to see us. Eldridge, DC, and I went to his office. The atmosphere was heavy, until we produced bags of various drugs recovered from Leary's visitors: some 20,000 hits, according to one count. Hoffman's jaw dropped. Ever since the Learys' arrival, the Panthers had been watchful of the couple's American guests and systematically shook them down with body checks and baggage searches. We explained the difficulty of handling Leary and our hope that he would not be long in the country. Hoffman advised us to be careful, nothing more.

One day, thankfully, the Learys upped and left, with no warning. By chance, I was at the airport meeting someone and saw them walking swiftly, almost running, toward the departure hall. We smiled and waved at each other.

Rosemary had told me that she was in contact with a doctor in Eastern Europe whom she hoped would rebuild her tubes so that she could conceive. Tim was as tired of us as we were of him, and wanted to move on. His dislike of me and of DC was manifest. He was more circumspect with Eldridge. On one occasion he monitored an LSD trip for Eldridge and Malika. She told me afterward, "Leary yelled at me: 'Go to it, Malika, turn on! Make love!'" Her sardonic reply: "I don't need pills for that."

Eldridge had met Leary in the States. His immediate reaction, when he first saw him again in Algiers, was to tell me that he had aged considerably and was intellectually diminished. More troublesome, it had been rumored for some time that Leary was not to be trusted. It was known that his research, in his Harvard professorship days, had put him in contact with the Central Intelligence Agency. In 1974, after spending time in Switzerland and briefly in Afghanistan, he was "kidnapped" by US narcotics agents in Kabul and forcibly shipped back to the US, where he was put under arrest. He provided the FBI with a full account of his escape from San Luis Obispo with the Weather Underground, his sojourn in Algeria, and events thereafter, and gave the DEA information on people he had dealt with in the past, leading to several arrests—including, briefly, that of his own lawyer.

In September 1974, an organization called People Investigating Leary's Lies (PILL) held a conference in San Francisco that was attended by Leary's son Jack and his now-former wife Rosemary, as well as a number of prominent personalities including Allen Ginsburg, Dick Gregory, Jerry Rubin, and William Kunstler. Leary was called a "liar," a "cop informant," and, in Jerry Rubin's words, a "paranoid schizophrenic."

Leary wrote several books that include his take on the Algerian experience, including *Confessions of a Hope Fiend* (1973) and *Flashbacks* (1989). They contain delirious, lie-packed fantasies of his Algerian interlude.

Building the Party

At this time, the International Section's main conduit for communication with Panther chapters, other organizations, and the media in the US was via film. The heavy, wide-band TV tapes in black-and-white had poor sound quality and jumpy images, and were expensive to ship.

A dramatic overhaul was to take place with the arrival from Paris, during the winter of 1970–71, of Carole and Paul Roussopoulos and their Sony half-inch Portapak. The Portapak was a two-part, battery-powered system: the first handheld film camera in history, alongside a compact VTR (video tape recorder) for recording with immediate playback. It could be operated by one strong person, camera in the hands and VTR hanging from a shoulder strap, for recording sessions of up to half an hour. It became known as the "Guerrilla TV," the weapon against the establishment.

Eldridge was excited when he called me to come to the office in El Biar to see the Portapak in action, with the films Carole and Paul had shot in September 1970 in Palestinian training camps in the Middle East. For him, the Portapak was the tool that would reinject the Algiers Panthers and their programs, ideas, and activities into the US media circuit. It would be the launching pad for BPP chapters looking to Algiers for direction, an organizational medium of quality. He had to have one.

The Portapak first appeared in the US in 1965. There were probably no more than a half-dozen such sets in all of France. There was one, Carole and Paul knew, at the École des Beaux-Arts at the intersection of Rue Bonaparte and Quai Malaquais along the Seine in Paris—my old stomping grounds. Twenty years had gone by, but my memories were molded in bronze. I was able to describe the buildings in detail to Pete O'Neal, who immediately departed for the shops on rue Didouche Mourad to buy a pair of sneakers and soft cotton gloves. Eldridge supplied a ticket to Paris and Pete left to do his work.

Unfortunately, he came back empty-handed. For several nights running he scaled walls and sped softly along hallways, only to find the room that housed the video equipment sealed to the outside world and windowless. Pete's superior skills were to no avail. Eldridge would have to find a way to pay for a Portapak, which of course he did, with the help of his media contacts at the Chinese embassy.

A distribution circuit was developed. With the complicity of friends at Air France, the trajectory from Algiers to a TV news-room in the US could be completed within forty-eight hours, and to the support committees in Europe, overnight.

Ten thousand people were waiting for Huey Newton when he walked out of prison on August 5, 1970. The California Court of Appeals had overturned a voluntary manslaughter conviction in the case of a shootout between Newton and two police officers that had left one officer dead. A new trial awaited, but after three long years he was back on the streets, with the pharaoh-like stat-ure of a man who had vanquished his foes: the handsome militant and intellectual would now induct his followers in the destruc-tion of the "system."

During Newton's time in prison, the Party had exploded and transformed. It had become radicalized under Cleaver, the arti-san and leader of the Free Huey campaign. Its watchwords were socialism and revolutionary violence: "*Off the pigs!*" "*The sky's the limit!*" The original platform, emphasizing self-defense, had been placed on the back burner. From a few hundred members the party had mushroomed into an organization whose numbers not even the leadership could estimate. Panther chapters had emerged all over the country and the BPP newspaper was flour-ishing, as were the party's "soft" programs. Underground cadre

Charles and Mildred Klein, Brooklyn, NY, 1927.

Elaine Mokhtefi with Mary Lloyd and Jacques Savary, Paris, 1952.

Simone de Beauvoir and Jean-Paul Sartre, demonstrating against war in Algeria, Paris, 1961

Platoon of Algerian liberation army troops, Kabylie, 1962.

Founding members of FLN, 1954.
Rabah Bitat, Mostefa Ben Boulaïd,
Mourad Didouche, Mohamed Boudiaf,
Krim Belkacem, Larbi Ben M'Hidi.

Crowd welcoming Ahmed
Ben Bella, Algiers, 1962.

Algiers, July 5, 1962, Independence Day.

Elaine Mokhtefi with
Kathleen Cleaver.

Raymond (Masai) Hewitt, Julia Wright,
David Hilliard, Casbah, Algiers, 1969.

Stokely Carmichael, Elaine Mokhtefi, FLN representatives, Oran, 1967.

Eldridge Cleaver and Elaine
Mokhtefi, FLN headquarters,
1969.

Malika Ziri,
Algiers, 1970.

Charlotte and
Pete O'Neal
with newborn
son Malcolm,
at Panther
headquarters,
Algiers, 1971.

Miriam Makeba and Stokely Carmichael, Algiers, 1969.

Poster announcing Panafrican
Cultural Festival, 1969.

Frantz Fanon.

Cover of *The Black Panther*, 1970.

Elaine Mokhtefi and Eldridge Cleaver
with Chinese counselor, Panther
headquarters, Algiers, 1970.

Eldridge Cleaver, David Hilliard, Pete O'Neal with FLN representatives
in charge of liberation movements, Algiers, 1969.

Mokhtar and Elaine Mokhtefi, Algiers, 1972.

Elaine Mokhtefi, France, 2017.

were being trained, arms stocked. Cleaver had created a party that Newton barely recognized.

The FBI was also at work under COINTELPRO. During 1968 and 1969, thirty-one Panther offices in eleven states were attacked, searched, and ransacked in police raids. Militants were arrested and murdered. Informants were everywhere and conspiracy tactics reigned, with phony letters to Panther leaders detailing supposed treachery by friends and fellow militants. As FBI files reveal, Hoover's organization devoted considerable effort to the preparation of these fake documents, one of which— over Huey Newton's signature—would denounce Cleaver to President Boumediene.

In Algiers, life proceeded anxiously, but in the firm belief that Huey would steer the organization safely into the revolutionary future. There may have been as many as thirty Panthers and dependents awaiting the chairman's first moves. There is no doubt that he was their "beloved leader" in the noble sense of the term. In the meantime, a new apartment in the workers' neighborhood of Bab El Oued became available, and single men were roomed there. The seaside house in Pointe Pescade and the Embassy in El Biar were home to the rest. The Cleavers cleared out of their bourgeois villa in Hydra. The Algiers Panthers were ready. In October, Newton applied for a passport for a trip to Algiers: request denied.

The atmosphere at the time was of revolutionary violence, typified by the actions of the Weather Underground which Newton, it was quickly realized, was unwilling to address. Newton was a poor public speaker. His delivery was soft and squeaky, interior, intellectual, and, on occasion, out of place. He was little understood by BPP activists who, faced with police harassment, prison, and assassination, needed to hear words of faith in the future, fighting words that inspired to overcome the odds—not lessons in philosophy.

Gradually, Newton's failures as a leader became clear. News reached Algiers that he had become dictatorial, curtained off by his lieutenants David Hilliard and his brother June. They were accused of living high off party funds, of using mob tactics to shake down local businesses in Oakland. Newton demanded complete control of party chapters. All decisions, all actions were to emanate from the Chairman, who then became "Supreme Commander," followed by "Servant of the People" and finally "Supreme Servant of the People."

He would stand for no criticism or upstaging; he expelled party members without preamble. He was living in an expensive penthouse, had taken over a nightclub (The Lamp Post), walked with a swagger stick, and was well along the downhill path to abusing cocaine and women, both furnished by the Hilliard brothers. For an eyewitness fact-check, Eldridge sent Connie Matthews to California, where she served as Newton's secretary and managed to send back increasingly disturbing reports.

When Newton, accompanied by David Hilliard and Connie Matthews, came east in February '71 to take part in rallies and Yale seminars in New Haven, Michael (Cetewayo) Tabor and Richard (Dhoruba) Moore of the New York 21 chapter met with him to air their grievances, but the encounter turned sour. East Coast Panthers, in disarray over pending court cases (including those of the New York 21, and the trial of Bobby Seale and Ericka Huggins for the murder of presumed informer Alex Rackley) were bristling. The New York 21 published an open letter of criticism of the Panther leadership for "tripping out, pseudo-machoism, arrogance, myrmidonism, dogmatism, regionalism, regimentation and fear." Newton expelled them from the party.

During this visit east, Connie Matthews, who had secretly married Tabor, was held prisoner by Newton and Hilliard in their New York hotel suite. To distract the two men so that Connie might make a getaway, Denise Oliver, a friend of Tabor's and a militant in the Young Lords, agreed to serve as decoy. Connie escaped; she, Tabor, and Moore resigned from the party and publicized their quarrel with Newton through a local radio station. "Enemies of the people," decreed Newton, expelling them from the party. Tabor, who was free on bail, and Matthews left immediately for Algiers via Canada. Denise Oliver, Connie's stand-in, was herself made a prisoner and forced into sex with a quasi-impotent Newton high on cocaine. She eventually came up with a ruse that allowed her to escape. Later that year in New York, I read her vivid text describing the ordeal.

Eldridge stayed in touch with Newton by telephone. Newton decided that they should both take part in the morning television show, "A.M. San Francisco," on February 26. On the show, host Jim Dunbar questioned Newton about his residence in a high-priced penthouse. At the end of the show, Cleaver seized the opportunity of the international phone-TV hook-up to demand that Newton reinstate the New York 21. The confrontation then descended into chaos. Newton refused. Cleaver proceeded to attack David Hilliard for his mismanagement of the BPP during the years Newton had been in prison, and called for his exclusion from the party. Newton halted the broadcast, and immediately phoned Algiers. The conversation ended with each man expelling the other from the Black Panther Party.

Eldridge Cleaver's demands, leveled at Newton during the joint interview, were not spontaneous. They had been discussed and calculated during meetings of the International Section beforehand. What was clear was that the BPP was in crisis. The group decided it was time to face Newton down.

That evening, Eldridge asked me to come by the Embassy to hear the recording of the television interview and telephone conversation with Newton. Newton's craziness on the phone and his refusal of rational discussion were painful to digest. Revenge for what he considered disloyalty was his overriding motivation:

> HN: You're a punk, you understand!
> EC: Say, Huey . . .
> HN: You're a punk!
> EC: I think you've lost your ability to reason.
> HN: You heard what I called you and that's what I feel about you now. You're a punk!
> EC: I wouldn't call you that.
> (Newton hangs up).[1]

The International Section immediately received the support of the East Coast Panthers and members throughout California, who had lost respect for "boss" Newton and his strong-arm tactics.

But Eldridge was far removed from the scene inside the United States and the wider destruction that had been wrought on left-wing activists and their organizations. After listening to the tape, I asked him, "Where does that leave you guys?" He was concerned about the split's effect on relations with the Algerian government. "That's of no worry, even if Huey tries to undermine you here," I assured him. "The Algerians won't get involved. It's not their problem, it's yours, Eldridge."

That became clear very quickly. Don Cox was preparing to travel to Kuwait to represent the BPP at the Second

International Symposium on Palestine when the Split occurred. Huey Newton called him immediately, wanting to know on whose side DC stood; they were old and tight comrades. "When I said I was opposed to him, he laughed in a high-pitched, excited manner and said he was going to 'crush' me." A few days later, Robert "Spider" Webb, DC's comrade and sidekick, was killed in Harlem. To quote DC, Huey "lashed out with megalomaniacal, perverted rage and ordered the assassination of Spider, just to hurt me, in order to avenge his injured, bloated ego."[2]

Internecine warfare continued. The group in Algiers, informed after the fact, was powerless to stop it. The ignominious murder of Bill Seidler in Philadelphia on March 18, 1971, was, for DC and Barbara Easley, the Seidlers' "adopted" daughter, an assassination. Seidler and his wife Miriam, an elderly Jewish couple, radicals whose clothing store and home had always been open to the Panthers, had served as relays for the distribution in the US of film tapes from Algiers. Miriam Seidler saw the assassin enter the shop and go directly to the rear where her husband was going over the books: "Put that thing down," she heard Bill say. The assassin aimed, fired, and exited. The press reported that Bill Seidler was the victim of a "hold-up." The investigation was summary. Miriam's testimony went unheard.

In March, Cleaver made a last-ditch attempt to mend the fences separating Algiers and Huey Newton. He pleaded with Newton to come to Algiers. Newton replied: "If I come over there I will only come over to kill you, Eldridge."

"Okay, brother. Come on over here and kill me."

Algeria Nationalizes

Two days before the Split, on February 24, 1971, Houari Boumediene announced the nationalization of French oil and gas holdings. All previous concessions became on that day 51 percent Algerian-owned. With the exception of the French company Total, they all pulled out of the country. The same decrees imposed state control over foreign mining, manufacturing, insurance, and agricultural companies.

Further, Boumediene outlined a three-stage agrarian reform. The first stage, from January 1972 to June 1973, would include the nationalization and redistribution of public lands, property inherited from the former French colonial administration, communal land, tribal land, and land held by religious entities (*habous*). The great beneficiaries of the new laws were the poor peasants, the fellahin.

During the second stage, from June 1973 to June 1975, partial nationalization and redistribution of absentee landowner estates and large-scale properties and palm groves would go into effect. The third stage would cover the nationalization of public pasture lands used by herdsmen.

The Panthers, who paid little attention to Algerian politics, missed the significance of the new decrees. Even with their increasing knowledge of French, they did not keep up with the French-language press. Colleagues sent them clippings from American newspapers. On television, they watched the international newscasts. DC set up short-wave connections to keep in touch with news from the States directly. Their principal interest in local policy concerned American interests in Algeria. They would later editorialize on their suspicions of increased American presence in the country—the underlying fear being that the

Algerian government would sell them short in order to obtain oil and gas contracts from American companies.

New "Wheels"

The Panthers' German support group paid for a brand-new minibus for the Algiers contingent, to be collected from the Volkswagen factory in Hanover. By then I was the only person in their entourage who could travel legally in Europe and had a proper driver's license.

Two days after the party split, I took a plane to Geneva and went on to Hanover by train. In possession of the purchase receipt, the transaction was quickly concluded, but I had to adjust immediately to driving what seemed to me a ten-ton truck and exit the factory. I made it to the autobahn and kept to the minimum speed permitted. It was illegal to crawl. Crossing the border into France near Strasbourg, I made it to Paris, where I spent the night. The next morning I began the daylong drive to Marseille, where, the following afternoon, the minibus and I boarded the ferry for the overnight trip to Algiers.

Coming to Algiers from the sea is one of the most spine-tingling travel experiences in the world. In the early morning light, the view from the water of the wall of white Moorish dwellings, the Casbah, is like gazing at a shimmering desert mirage—and as unreal. The entire city sweeps upward and envelops the mountain behind it in a blaze of light from the east.

The minibus made a sensational entrance. I can still see it in my mind's eye, parked in front of the Embassy in El Biar and whizzing around town with its load of Black Panthers, friends, and consorts.

෨෬

In April 1971, the FLN forwarded an invitation to the Algiers Panthers from the People's Republic of the Congo for an international conference in support of the liberation struggle of the Portuguese colonies of Angola, Mozambique, and Guinea-Bissau, to take place in Brazzaville. The visit was later extended to include the May Day celebrations.

This was the Panthers' chance to discover and identify with Black Africa at a time that was, for them, one of confusion and uncertainty. It was a dream come true and they were elated. Except for Kathleen who, as a child, had lived in Liberia and visited Sierra Leone with her diplomatic-corps parents, none of them had ever set foot in sub-Saharan, Black Africa. Michael (Cetewayo) Tabor, Denise Oliver (who came from New York for the trip), Kathleen, and Eldridge composed the delegation, to which Bill Stephens, the photographer and video operator, was added as soon as he collected the equipment.

Plane-hopping across Africa to reach Brazzaville was not Eldridge's idea of fun: Algiers to Bamako, Bamako to Abidjan, Abidjan to Libreville, and finally Brazzaville. The possibility of Cetewayo and Eldridge being taken into custody at a stopover and extradited as fugitives from US justice was a constant concern. Panic-stricken during the overnight in Bamako, Mali, they contacted the Algerian ambassador, who reassured them that their Algerian documents and tickets would get them through safely. All went without a hitch, but on the way back it was arranged for them to fly from Brazzaville to Moscow nonstop, then Moscow to Algiers.

After the conference and the May Day celebrations, the delegation visited Pointe Noire, notorious for its historic role as a departure point for slave ships bound for the New World. The descendants of the men and women who had clawed the sands of those beaches, in their desperate struggle to hold on to African soil, had returned in the form of American Panthers. Eldridge projected that the film they would put together following their trip would be called "We Have Come Back!"

From Pointe Noire the group crossed into Cabinda, an enclave of Angola, currently at war against the Portuguese colonial regime. They were welcomed at an MPLA (Popular Movement for the Liberation of Angola) guerrilla camp in "liberated territory."

The government of Congo-Brazzaville defined itself as revolutionary: Marxist-Leninist in inspiration, and functioning within the Soviet orbit. The Panthers were enthralled with Ange Diawara—theoretician, political commissar of the People's Army, and government minister—whom they understood was their sponsor for the trip. By the time they met with President Marien Ngouabi at the end of their visit, they had decided to open a Panther information office in Brazzaville.

On their return to Algiers in mid-May, Eldridge told me the Panthers would be moving to the Congo. They were presenting a formal request to open an office, and would gradually transfer the whole operation. I was flabbergasted: connections between Algiers and the States were frustrating enough, but from Brazzaville, what did Eldridge expect? "How will you relate?" "We felt at home there," was his reply.

They never received an answer to their request for status as a liberation movement in the Congo. In February 1972, Ange Diawara was on the run, having led a failed coup against President Ngouabi. In 1973, he was captured and executed.

Eldridge had a reputation for throwing fat on the fire. It had worked in the States, where he scorched his audiences with phrases like "fuck Ronald Reagan" and "pussy power." He was good at turning up the heat, skewering the enemy with nicknames of "Mafioso Alioto" or "Hitler Hoover." His slogans for action ignited cheering crowds: "Off the pigs!" "Free Huey!" "Pick up the gun!" He learned that he could pull the crowd with him, no matter how gross or how violent his rhetoric. It was awesome usage of the shock technique.

His most famous exploit in this genre took place at the College of the Pacific, a Bay Area school. The women who came to Eldridge's talk were studying to be nuns, wearing habits and fingering rosaries. He suddenly cried out, "I'm going to liberate you. I'm going to lead you in a chant . . . Now here's the first stanza. I'll say it and you repeat it: FUCK RONALD REAGAN!" According to David Hilliard, after some hesitation and a few trial runs, "the scene's an exorcism. Eldridge has proven himself true. The nuns are free; they are laughing and clapping and repeating the chant."[3]

When Eldridge employed similar tactics in Africa, though, he often courted disaster. In the Congo, his official speech at the conference turned into a forthright attack on the Soviet Union, "revisionist" countries, and revisionism in general. "The rationing of aid to peoples of color shows the racist nature of many of the so-called socialist countries," he warned the international congress. Could he have been ignorant of the cold facts behind the organization of the conference he was attending, or did he consider himself cool enough, powerful enough, to bring the crowd along? After all, this conference had been financed and staffed by the World Federation of Democratic Youth, a Communist-bloc youth organization headquartered in Budapest. By the same token, the Congolese government was heavily indebted to the USSR. In the middle of the night following his speech, Eldridge and Kathleen were suddenly moved from their hotel room, "for their own good," it seems.

In his application to the government to transfer headquarters to Brazzaville, Eldridge emphasized that time was of the essence, because "enemies are moving to destroy our base in Algiers." He was assuming that Marien Ngouabi would let pass his broadside against the Congo's Soviet-bloc sponsors, and that the Congolese authorities would accede to his request without consulting the Algerian government.

With the Split, the Algiers Panthers withdrew from the BPP and stopped referring to themselves as the International Section of the Black Panther Party. Their goal was now to become a clearinghouse for information and contact among leftist groups of different origins. To this end, they would edit a newspaper for distribution in the US and Europe. They named their operation the Revolutionary People's Communication Network (RPCN).

On October 25, 1971, Kathleen and Jessica Scott Weinrich—a Panther militant in Germany active with Black soldiers at Ramstein, the American air base—along with the two Cleaver children and me, boarded a Swissair flight in Geneva bound for New York. We were taking off for a round-the-US speaking tour to launch the RPCN and raise money for its operation.

When Eldridge asked me to be part of the delegation, I replied in the affirmative without hesitation. Adding a white woman to the group was his way of portraying a principle in black and white. He was also acquiring someone whom he could trust with handling money and organization of the tour; he no longer had an open pool of handlers at his fingertips in the States. For me, it was a challenge, a welcome opportunity to test the American scene for myself. And I was flattered.

Kathleen was relaxed, glad to be on mission, more lighthearted than I'd seen her for many a month or year. I was excited too, but at base nervous and wary. We were wandering into dangerous territory. Now that we were on our way, nagging queries were banging inside my head. How would I react? More important, what did I have to say? Who was I? It had been twenty years since I left the United States for Europe and Africa. Blacks were totally ghettoized back then. I had witnessed their radicalization from a distance. And the backlash, the murderous aggression of the state against the Black Panthers and other progressive groups—I felt out of my depth and unsure of myself. Would I be able to wing it?

Black America had just received a death knell from Attica prison in upstate New York. Thirty-three prisoners and ten guards were assassinated when Governor Nelson Rockefeller ordered the New York State Police and the National Guard to crush a prisoner uprising. The insurrection had started as a protest against the murder of George Jackson at San Quentin, then transformed into a demand for improved living conditions.

Former SNCC leader H. Rap Brown had been arrested the week before our arrival, following a shootout with the police at a bar on the Upper West Side of New York. Kathleen was concerned; she had worked with him in SNCC and the BPP. Hundreds of thousands of marchers had just descended on Washington to demand an end to the Vietnam War. And on the day of our arrival, the United Nations ejected the Republic of China (Taiwan), and welcomed the People's Republic into its ranks after a twenty-two-year boycott engineered by the United States.

In the plane Kathleen held Joju on her lap. Maceo, a little over two by now, sat between us. When we arrived over JFK, the plane circled, dipping up and around for so long that the passengers were unnerved. The pilot announced that he was prepared to land but authorization was being denied. He persisted but the tower kept us hovering over the airport. Finally, we were informed that we were rerouting to Boston, the reason being "fog" over New York.

It took little time for us to seize on the real explanation for the detour. Hundreds of Panther supporters had crowded the New York airport waiting for Kathleen to disembark, but the FBI had fabricated a scenario to deprive her of the spotlight. We landed in Boston where the only people in attendance were a few hurried journalists and the FBI. An agent appeared in the arrival hall, waved a photo in Jessica's face, and shouted: "Gwen Patterson, you are under arrest!" The real Gwen, who with her husband James (Akili) had hijacked a plane to Cuba a few years back, was living quietly in Algiers, a fact that was surely not unknown to the FBI.

In the time it takes to snap your fingers, Kathleen was on top of the situation. She dug into her bag, wrote down a telephone number, and told me to get to a phone. The number was for a lawyer in New York, to whom I gave a rundown of the situation. He said he would contact a Boston colleague who would meet Kathleen at the federal jail. Jessica was pushed into the agents' car. Kathleen followed by taxi.

I held Joju tight in one arm and took Maceo by the hand. We joined the other passengers going into Boston to the airline's hotel. With the lawyer's help, Jessica was released later that night—no apology—and the following morning Swissair put us on a flight to New York.

A small group came to LaGuardia to greet us: Denise Oliver, Janet Cyril, and Elbert "Big Man" Howard—Panther stalwarts. They took us into the city and set us up in the apartment Denise had rented on 102nd Street, between Broadway and West End Avenue. It was a two-bedroom ground-floor unit with a back-yard. On the north side of the street, across from the entrance to the building, a large white van remained stationed for the two months we were in the States. To lay plans and name contacts, we strode around the backyard and whispered, or ducked into the bathroom and turned on the shower.

Those first few days in the States gave me a new perspective on Kathleen. I had known her in Algiers as vindictive, jealous, subordinate to Eldridge's whims and decisions. I had witnessed her mean side. Here, she was clearheaded, reacting with speed and efficiency to every situation. Her on-stage personality was militant, while not lacking in charm and occasional humor. At home in her role, she even managed to cooperate with me. I once challenged Eldridge on his treatment of her, the verbal abuse and the physical violence we all observed. "She's a battered woman, Eldridge. Why do you treat her like that?" Even his male colleagues had objected, and called a meeting to put him on the skillet. His answer to me: "Some people demand to be treated like that."

Kathleen and Jessica took off immediately for California with a full agenda: to introduce the children to their Cleaver grand-mother and family, and support Elmer "Geronimo" Pratt, whose trial was coming up in Los Angeles, plus a speaking engagement at UCLA.

Geronimo had been framed by the feds, accused of a murder in Los Angeles at the very moment he was attending a Panther executive meeting in Oakland, 300 miles away. Newton, Seale, and Hilliard refused to testify at his trial, because he had opposed them and supported Cleaver following the Split. Years later, they would state their "regret" for not defending him.

Kathleen needed no prodding; she defended Geronimo firmly, but her testimony alone was insufficient. Johnnie Cochran, Pratt's lawyer, praised Kathleen for her courage: testifying had its dangers in the climate reigning in California in those times.

Geronimo spent twenty-seven years in prison. His lawyers denounced the numerous irregularities of his trial, including a state's witness who was a paid police informer but was never identified as such. It took until 1999 to overturn his conviction. He was awarded 4.5 million dollars by the state of California and the federal government. Shortly thereafter, he married the Cleavers' daughter, Joju. They went to live in Tanzania, where Geronimo died in 2011.

The same little Joju who was one year old when I held her in my arms the night her mother and I landed in Boston.

As soon as Kathleen left for California, I worked with Denise, Janet, and Big Man, who had been the first editor of the Panther newspaper in Oakland in 1968, to organize the tour, contacting schools and universities, Panthers, and African-American community organizations. I operated from public phone booths, supplying a code number for calls that would be charged to someone whose name and address I did not know. I burned the wires with hundreds of calls around the United States and to Algiers.

My parents were still living in Ridgefield. I spent a few days with them, being careful to underplay the tour I was about to embark on with Kathleen. The dangers we faced were too real. My mother Mildred had met both Kathleen and Eldridge in 1970 in Algiers. She had traveled with Kathleen from Algiers to London to New York when she returned to the States after that trip. In London, when the airport police forced Kathleen into a controlled waiting area, Mildred had stayed by her and run errands for food and drink.

When Kathleen and Jessica returned from California, we headed for Stony Brook University, then to Boston, where we were received by groups at Brandeis, MIT, and Tufts. The next stop was the University of Buffalo. The large amphitheater was packed to the rafters with students. Kathleen arrived on stage with her long-legged stride, big Afro, and black leather jacket. She stopped, scanned the house, looked the students in the eye, and raised her fist: "Power to the people!" she bellowed. The majority-white audience received her thunder and roared in return. Fists lifted in acknowledgment. She talked revolution and discussed the situation in Black communities across the country. She explained the Split and introduced the RPCN, calling for support. Bill Stephens had joined us with the Portapak video and recorder and was filming. We were surrounded and cheered. Jessica and I passed the hat—or was it a duffel bag?

We flew to Detroit. Motown looked like Dresden after the infamous Allied bombing. In 1967, Detroit had been the center of the most violent racial insurrection in the history of the United States. Forty-three people were killed, twenty-five by the army and seventeen by the police. The scars of the weeklong battle that pitted the city's Black population against not only the Detroit police and the US Army, but the Michigan State Police and the National Guard, were deep, and fully on display four years later: neighborhoods were burned out, empty of inhabitants. I remember driving miles to find a pharmacy for Kathleen.

Then, in 1970, the police attacked two men selling Panther literature on the sidewalk, triggering a six-hour standoff between the police and the population that ended in the death of a cop and the arrest of fifteen Panthers. Local activities had somehow been maintained: breakfast for children, food distribution to needy families, busing to nearby prisons. With local militants, we discussed the situation within the party and arranged to return to Detroit for a blowout public meeting with Kathleen before leaving the States.

In Chicago we met with a group of very young teenage militants, inspired by the Panthers: a new generation, more restrained than their idols, cautious and less flashy. They stated that they were ready to give their lives for a better future for their people. It was there that I heard a young man declare: "If my parents have to go, they have to go"—as in die.

We stopped in Yellow Springs, Ohio, at Antioch College. There I made my debut on the platform with Kathleen, discussing political organizations and liberation movements around the world.

"England, Portugal, and South Africa are waging war in Africa at this very moment against freedom fighters in Zimbabwe, Namibia, South Africa, and all the Portuguese colonies. The colonial powers will go to any lengths to maintain power over the people and the resources of Africa." I described the guerrilla movements against fascist regimes in Central and South America, as well as in the war in Vietnam. The audience was stunned. Their knowledge of the Third World was nil. City and local newspapers revealed little of events outside the United States and of the struggles of whole peoples. News was incidental, superficial, never enlightening.

In Kansas City we were received by Pete and Charlotte O'Neal's families. They were old acquaintances from Algiers, where they had come to visit their exiled children. Community and church events had been prepared. Kathleen spoke at Park College in Parkville, Missouri. When we moved on to Nashville, Jessica left us to visit her family. We flew to Tallahassee for a rally at Florida State University, where leather-clad guards fanned out behind us on the stage. At Reverend Steele's church downtown, Kathleen's appearance followed that of the radical lawyer William Kunstler. We held workshops: I led one on media and one on liberation movements. There was a stir when someone tried to break up the "white woman's" workshops. That effort was the only open attack against my presence on the delegation during the tour. Kathleen was firm: I was a militant in Algiers, and the RPCN was a meeting place for revolutionaries of every background.

From Tallahassee, we went to Jacksonville for a day, then back to Detroit where we held a successful Panther-style rally and took over the comfortable house of US congressman Charles Diggs, absent in Washington, and whose nephew Phil Garner was a Panther. Our next stop was to be Northfield, Minnesota, for a speech at liberal Carlton College. It had been one of the first engagements I had arranged, and our fee was a welcome $2,000.

We sat around the large living room of the Diggs house with several Detroit Panthers. The conversation turned to the Minnesota meeting; our hosts became increasingly admonitory about our safety, describing every possible trick in the FBI bag to endanger Kathleen's life and stop the tour. "We have no contacts at Carlton College. There'll be no protection for you." Their dogmatic conclusion: "Cancel the trip!" At that point, I left them and went to bed, only to be awakened later in the night by Eldridge, calling from Algiers, who wanted to know what was going on, why had we canceled, what Kathleen was doing. Who were those dudes in the house? Had we been smoking pot?

Yes, we'd smoked some pot. No, I couldn't believe these guys had any kind of inside information as to the situation on a university campus in little Northfield, Minnesota. However, they had got to Kathleen, who, tired and distraught from so much traveling and tension, had given in to their exhortations. "She's scared," I admitted.

We went back to New York. Kathleen left unaccompanied for a speaking engagement in New Orleans. Her mother had to go back to work, so she flew on to Washington to pick up Maceo and Joju and left for Algiers. I remained in New York for another three weeks, during which time Janet, Denise, Big Man and I designed, wrote, typed up, illustrated, printed, and distributed a new Panther newspaper called *Babylon*. We used a special typesetter that could justify the right-hand margin and set columns, all very slow and time-consuming. We holed up in the 102nd Street apartment night and day, eating Big Man's Southern cooking and corn bread. Together we formed an amazing editorial team. We played and replayed The Last Poets. I typed in time to their rap: "There won't be no commercials when the Revolution comes . . ."

I wrote one article on the Algerian FLN's set-up in France during the liberation war: a system based on a three-person pyramid; one group leader and two base members. I wrote another on Fanon, as well as many fillers. We sent off the first copy to Eldridge in Algiers. He had already objected to the title, *Babylon*, but we held firm. He wanted it to be called *Grapevine*, in remembrance of the strategies of plantation Blacks to keep one another informed in the times of slavery. He felt *Grapevine* was more adapted to the situation of Panthers in 1971. He also objected to the tone of a number of articles: "Too much like reading the *New York Times*," he quipped.

With Big Man's lists of Panther selling points and chapters, we shipped *Babylon* out across the country and dropped copies all over New York. It was a successful operation, but we knew that it would be difficult to continue with so little staff and finance.

It was time for me to leave for Algiers and get back to work. I made a reservation by telephone from the apartment for a flight from New York to London and went to the airport. The white van was still standing across the street from the 102nd Street building.

At the airport, the line for tickets and seat allocation was long and slow. As I drew closer to the counter, I observed two men in suits, ties and overcoats watching and waiting as passengers approached. They were discreetly checking people's names as passengers neared the counter. I had a firm premonition that the person they were waiting for was me. I left the line, quit the airport, and took a taxi back to the city. I told the comrades at the apartment that I would make a run for it another day. Big Man was sure it was the telephone call for a reservation that had alerted them to my departure.

Two days later, on December 19, 1971, I went directly to the airport without a reservation and bought a ticket for London. There was no one waiting at the airlines counter to oversee ticket sales. In London I changed planes for Algiers.[4]

Back at my apartment, I flaked out and slept for twenty-four hours before going to El Biar to meet with Eldridge and DC, who were anxious to know what I'd seen and what my thoughts were.

How to put it? The groups I had met and talked with were the remnants of an organization. Their leaders were either dead, in prison, on the run, or on the defensive. Those who rejected the Oakland gang were on their own. The only new group I'd seen was the far-out teenagers in Chicago. Our meetings at universities were organized by students, not Panthers, and were not a solid indication of the strength of revolutionary groups on campus. People had come out to hear Kathleen more out of curiosity than conviction or a need to get back into the struggle. People in the Black community still participated in local programs, like breakfast for children and food distribution; they would come out on call. But the dynamics had changed. I told them that I didn't feel the sparks of revolution. Fresh leadership and new or renewed energy were required, and those could not be sourced from Algiers. Eldridge and DC were both in their late thirties. I suddenly saw them as survivors. I imagine they felt the same.

Back to Work

At the Ministry of Information, Behja, Zohra, and Mahmoud, my colleagues on the team editing the new, slick international magazine, were waiting for me. The mock layout had arrived.[5] Our first trial issue would soon be on the block to show to Mohamed Benyahia, minister of information. A second issue was already underway. From then on, our small group was nailed to that office. We knew we had a winner. We called it *Sud* (South), a way of indicating our determination to talk about Third World problems and concepts, as opposed to those of the colonialist and imperialist North.

One evening in early February 1972, as Behja and I left the ministry in my Mini, she hailed someone coming out of the bakery across the street and told me to stop. I stepped on the brakes and Behja wound down her window. The man carrying a baguette who doubled over to greet us through that open window was Mokhtar Mokhtefi, a liberation war veteran with whom Behja had worked at the Ministry of Agriculture right after independence. I had heard his name many times over the years from Behja, Zohra, and others, always with respect for his character and intelligence. He was already familiar to me.

Mokhtar called Behja the next day, suggesting she organize a party and invite him, me, and anyone else she desired. The party was just a party, but for me it is the unshakable turning point of my life. Behja made her signature dish, chicken with *citrons confits*. We drank La Cuvée du Président, red wine from the orchards along the coast. Someone put on records and we danced. As people were leaving, Mokhtar told me he had no transportation: "Can you drop me off on your way home?"

He was a beautiful man: over six feet tall, with large dark eyes that addressed one directly, an aquiline nose, and longish hair that covered his head in ringlets. He was intelligent and clear-spoken: he said things so that they would be understood, not buried in terms that diluted meaning. He had a sense of humor and of dignity. I had often heard from my friends that he was brave and principled. I have marveled ever since at the wonder of our encounter. Can I say we were made for each other? Is that too banal a thought? It is what I believe.

When I first met Mokhtar, he was employed by Sonatrach, the giant Algerian oil company, the most powerful economic element of a country totally dependent for survival—then as now—on its gas and oil. Mokhtar had been sent to France by the company to complete his studies and receive training in international finance. He had an office on one of the upper floors of Sonatrach's headquarters and—a sure indication of status—all French and Algerian newspapers and magazines of interest were deposited daily on his desk.

But no work was ever detailed to him. He twiddled his thumbs and read the press. Slippery colleagues, oafs or hacks most probably, fearful of competition, saw to it that he remained idle. It was one of our essential topics of conversation over drinks and dinner, a desperate problem that had invaded almost every segment of government. One day he got up, left that office and never went back. Thereafter, he took consultancy jobs, on contract, refusing anything that meant becoming a civil servant. It was not the first, nor the last, blow to his faith and ideals.

I had known Mokhtar for just a few weeks and was already heavily involved with him, spending most evenings at his small apartment on rue Enfantin, one short street away from my office at the Ministry of Information. Either he did the shopping for dinner or I rushed to the butcher's or the baker's on my way to his place. We already had this routine going when Eldridge asked me to go to Paris, to work with Carole and Paul Roussopoulos on a film they were putting together about the Algiers Panthers. Eldridge was mistrustful of the couple's knowledge of the United States, and wanted another eye on the project. Aimed at an American audience, the film was intended to launch the Revolutionary People's Communication Network in Eldridge's Babylon.

I spent several days and nights at the Roussopouloses' apartment on rue de l'Odéon, reeling and editing the Portapak tapes with them. Carole and Paul were self-taught recording and montage technicians. When I complimented them on their professional proficiency, they balked: "We're not professionals, we're militants. It's all the difference." Unfortunately, the footage we were working with lacked the spectacular sequences of earlier Panther films based on a variety of dynamic, charismatic live events. This one was largely talk and conversations, filmed in interior settings. Despite our efforts, Eldridge judged the video too sober and artistic, lacking in fire. I don't think it was ever shown in public.

A few days before I was to leave Paris, Connie Matthews arrived for a meeting at the Mutualité, a hall on the Left Bank often used for political rallies. She updated an overflowing crowd of enthusiastic supporters on the Split and the state of Panther affairs in the US and Algiers. The night before Connie and I were due to leave, Kathleen Cleaver arrived from Scandinavia. The three of us went together to Orly for the flight to Algiers.

As we proceeded to the airline boarding gate, Connie and Kathleen were stopped by the police and hustled into an office in the boarding area where they were given official notification that they were no longer welcome in France. The police asked Air Algérie to delay our flight's departure. They wanted to ensure that the two women left the country. We ran for it.

6

Hijackers

For the Panthers, money was a constant worry. How to keep an establishment of several dozen adults and their children alive with the small stipend from the FLN and Eldridge's earnings from his writing, seriously hampered by US government restrictions? Once again I tried to convince him to amend his agreement with Beverly Axelrod for the royalties from *Soul on Ice*.

"Come on, Eldridge, times are changing."

"No way," he insisted stubbornly.

Before the end of the year, however, he would have a change of heart and attempt to quash the Axelrod contract. By then he was ready to leave his past where it was—in the past.

A source of help, however, seemingly appeared out of the blue. Midday on June 3, 1972, I received a phone call from the central office of the National Liberation Front. A rushed voice announced that the man now responsible for liberation movements, Djelloul Malaika, was on the line. Malaika too was in a hurry, no *salamalecs*: "Get Eldridge Cleaver and be at Dar El Beïda Airport by 6 p.m. A plane hijacked in the United States is heading for Algiers," he said.

The Panthers were already savvy. DC had been monitoring the hijacking by short-wave since the middle of the night. He had followed the plane from Los Angeles to Seattle to San Francisco, where half of the eighty-seven passengers were released and a jet capable of crossing the Atlantic was made ready. That aircraft set down in New York, freed the remaining passengers and, with only the hijackers on board, was now approaching Spain and the Mediterranean in preparation for landing in Algiers.

In high spirits, Eldridge, DC, Pete O'Neal, and I drove to the airport in the Panther minibus. We knew the hijackers had amassed a ransom of $500,000, and could only imagine that they had hijacked the plane in order to collect and deliver those precious dollars to the International Section of the Black Panther Party. Expecting to welcome old comrades, the three men conjectured as to who would have designed and executed this audacious project.

A group of Algerian officials, all smiles, was waiting for us. They were from the country's top-level security apparatus, the party hierarchy, and the Ministry of Foreign Affairs. I had never seen Algerian functionaries so solicitous: they were counting on us to get them through this adventure without mishap. They had imagined a scenario and quickly distributed our roles. Since the air pirates had demanded that Eldridge Cleaver be at the airport on their arrival, he and his two comrades were directed to board the plane on landing and lead the pirates and crew out safely. I was to go to the control tower and do whatever talking and interpreting was necessary with the people on the plane.

As we stepped onto the tarmac and walked towards the tower, I was behind the Panthers and could see that they were all three armed. They carried themselves straight and ready, their bodies rolling in step, Eldridge in the middle, their right-side pockets bulging. There was no doubt that the Algerians on the tarmac also saw that the Panthers were "packing." If a shootout there was, they would be on the front line.

We waited near the tower. A few minutes before 7 p.m. we spotted the aircraft approaching, preparing to land. All of a sudden, Djelloul Malaika came running out of the air-control building, shouting: "They're not your people, they're hers," pointing at me. "They're Weathermen. Wait here. We're going on board ourselves."

For the authorities present, the hijackers had changed color from black to white. With a twitch of a magic wand, they were no longer seen as threatening: this the Algerians could handle. It was an amazing conclusion, based on ignorance but also on the unconfessable need to take over from an organization they didn't understand and weren't sure they knew how to deal with.

The four of us stood on the tarmac and watched the plane land. As soon as the motors were cut and the gangway hit the ground, a dozen uniformed men in riot gear scurried inside the aircraft. Silence followed. No shots. We waited, relieved, as the Algerians came out again. After a pause that seemed too long, at the top of the gangway there appeared a skinny, long-legged African American, wearing a wrinkled American army uniform and steel-rimmed glasses, and a slender young white woman with long reddish-brown hair, both somewhat dazed. Their descent from the doorway of the plane was laborious: they wobbled a little, unsure of themselves. The vision is as fresh now as on that day a half-century ago: Willie Roger Holder and Cathy Kerkow, twenty-three and twenty years old.

We watched as the Algerians met them at the bottom of the gangway and took the money bags from Roger's unsuspecting hands. Everyone descended from the tower and we all moved into the airport's arrival lounge for special guests, *le salon d'honneur*.

Our first exchanges with Roger and Cathy were warm and congratulatory. We all embraced. Roger was giddy: he showed us the inside of the attaché case that he had convinced the aircrew held a bomb he was capable of detonating if his demands were not met. It contained two books on interpreting the zodiac, a shaving kit, and a short piece of copper wire whose other end was attached to a ring on Roger's left index finger. The nonexistent weapon had been powerful enough to propel the couple safely across the United States, the Atlantic Ocean, and the Mediterranean Sea in a stolen plane. Cathy giggled and told DC that she "had just come along for the ride."

Inside the airport lounge, a lot of people were milling about but nothing seemed to be happening. Maybe no one knew exactly what to do. It wasn't every day that a hijacked plane dropped down in Algiers with half a million dollars to give away. Finally, Eldridge and I sat down next to the table on which the bags of cash had been deposited and I posed the question to the head of Algerian security, Hadi Khediri: "What about the money?" I gestured toward Eldridge, meaning, "It was destined for the Panthers, *n'est-ce pas?*"

"It's in our safekeeping," Khediri replied. He could see we were upset. Pointing his finger at me, he added forcefully: "You know you can trust us." The pit of my stomach reacted with a lurch to Khediri's statement. Somehow my body realized, quicker than my head, that all was not well.

I remember Mohamed Aberkane, from the Ministry of Foreign Affairs, at Khediri's side. Aberkane, who had studied in the States, spoke fluent English, and I had assumed he would be the contact person with American officials in Algiers. Because of our stateside connection he and I had always had a cordial relationship, but that day I felt a grain of hostility. It didn't augur well for the money.

Roger and Cathy were taken to the Aletti, the elegant hotel in downtown Algiers. A few days later, the couple was turned over to the Panthers.

It was clear that the hijackers had no more connection to the Weathermen than they did to the Black Panthers. Roger had asked the tower to summon Eldridge to the airport but, as the plane began its descent into Algiers, he'd had second thoughts. He could not lie to the face of the Panther leader, so he changed his cloak to that of the Weathermen and announced that affiliation to the authorities on the ground.

Roger, now unemployed, had been a tank and helicopter gunner with the US Army in Vietnam. He was smart; he had handled the hijacking alone from start to finish. It was his brainchild. The *New York Times* described him as "a slim, cool black man in his twenties." According to the Western Airlines pilot, Bill Newell, "the hijacker was a highly intelligent man dissatisfied with his experiences in the Army."[1] Cathy worked in a massage parlor in San Diego.

At dinner one night in Algiers with Mokhtar and I, Roger drew us a copy of the diagram of a bomb that he had wagged in front of the pilots' noses. Cathy laughed and admitted she hadn't understood what was going on, but had pleaded with Roger that no one get hurt. She didn't learn until they hit Algiers that the famous black case contained neither bomb nor weapon, just a piece of copper wire attached to thin air.

On both planes they'd sat apart. For the pilots, he had prepared an elaborate yarn: he was an unwilling member of a group on board composed of three other men, one woman, three guns, and two more bombs. He said the others were from the Weather Underground, and that he had been coerced into cooperating: if he didn't, they threatened to harm his twin daughters, whom they had kidnapped from their mother's apartment in San Diego. Furthermore, he warned, one of them was high on LSD.

Over the plane's public-address system, he intermittently gave orders and bantered with his alleged collaborators. Roger was on stage and lapping it up, on a high, with an occasional joint to round things out. When, on arrival in New York, the last passengers left the plane, the crew saw that Roger's only accomplice had been little Cathy.

Perhaps the most startling aspect of the affair was that Algiers had not been Roger's original destination. His plan was bolder: he was going to grab a plane and rescue Angela Davis, then on trial in San Jose, California, and whisk her away to freedom by taking the plane to North Vietnam.

The day of the hijacking, the jury in the Angela Davis case had begun its deliberations. When Davis was summoned to the courtroom and told that a hijacking was underway with her as the air pirates' bounty, she was stunned and appalled. She convinced the judge that she had no connection whatsoever to this event. The jury was out, sequestered in a local hotel and not informed of the attempted raid. She would be acquitted.

Roger still had a plane and passengers to exchange for a heavy ransom, and was not ready to give himself up. His day of glory had arrived. To abandon the plan now was to surrender to humiliation, defeat—and prison. His record was already damning: he was a deserter from the US Army holding a dishonorable discharge.

He announced to the pilots that they were changing course and heading for Algiers.

Now Roger and Cathy had landed in Algeria. Their dollars were about to be returned to the airlines by the authorities, but they were free.

One of the fantasies Roger aired in his later years was that he and Cathy met President Houari Boumediene a few days after arrival, so that Boumediene could give them a quick look-over. The idea is absurd, as are many of the storybook scenes that Roger invented throughout his life. He died of an acute brain aneurysm in 2011; he was sixty-two years old. By then, the imaginative mastermind of that successful hijacking was a pill-popping addict with a shaky memory—a paranoid schizophrenic, according to some.[2]

I spent two months in Paris that summer of 1972, leaving after the skyjack affair. Mokhtar joined me for two extended stays. I introduced him to my Parisian pals. In September, I would be starting a new job teaching at the École de Journalisme of Algiers University.

The attractive international magazine that my working group spent months preparing had been scrubbed. Benyahia had become minister of higher education and scientific research, and Ahmed Taleb replaced him as minister of information. Taleb's cabinet director announced that *Sud* could only proceed if I were dropped from the team. Why? I never knew, though I did a line-up of the possibilities: American, foreigner, Jewish, female, spy, non-Arabic-speaking?

The cabinet director called our team together for a meeting. He spoke only in Arabic, which meant that neither Zohra, whose mother was French and who was brought up in France, nor I could follow what was being said. We all knew he spoke French, the language of our magazine. And I'd met his boss, Ahmed Taleb, when he spent several months in New York towards the end of the Algerian war for medical treatment. I had seen him numerous times in Algiers since independence, and had wandered the city streets with him. He had even confided in me about the women in his life. We talked politics: he was another one of those men who thought that he alone "understood" the Algerian people. Our relationship had always been pleasant and at times close. As for foreigners, Taleb had himself married a woman from the Middle East.

So many people took any American outside the United States to be in the CIA that it became no more than a gratuitous accusation, mud-slinging, best to ignore. If the issue was my Jewish ancestors, it would have been the first time, in all the years I lived in Algeria, that this was used against me.

When our group's leader, Mahmoud Tlemsani, met alone with Taleb's cabinet director and was asked to dismiss me, he refused. All three colleagues resigned from the ministry in solidarity, and the magazine dropped dead.

7

A Wedding and Its Consequences

During this period, Behja Bensalem and Zohra Sellami were my closest colleagues at the Ministry of Information. It was with them that I worked and played in and out of the office: Behja, a very smart and sensitive woman with a small oval face and penetrating eyes set behind large round glasses, and Zohra, an adorable, sharp-witted woman who packed a wallop. Behja had lingering ways; she was warm and affectionate. Zohra, pretty as a picture, was a "stomper" who expressed her opinions with a hiss of four-letter words. From 1968, when we began organizing the Pan-African Cultural Festival, to our departure from the ministry in 1972, we pulled together. After *Sud* was closed down, we each had to scramble for a new way forward. Behja went back to college to complete her degree in sociology. Mahmoud went to work in the Algerian film industry. I became a professor of journalism. And Zohra's life would take an epic turn.

One ordinary day, Zohra was invited to tea by an acquaintance, an older woman. She told us how surprised she was when their conversation became highly personal, with questions she would not have expected; she had the feeling she was being interviewed. Indeed she was, as were several other young single women in Algiers at about the same time. Not long afterward, she was contacted by Mohamed Hadj-Smaine, the former minister of justice and ally of former president Ahmed Ben Bella, who had been incarcerated since the 1965 coup d'état. Hadj-Smaine was the only person other than Ben Bella's immediate family authorized to visit him in his prison residence. He explained to Zohra that he was entrusted with a delicate mission of unusual import. Ben Bella, in captivity, had received authorization from Boumediene to marry.

"Would you accept to be his bride?" was the straightforward question he put to the astounded Zohra.

She was blown over but kept her cool. She asked permission to meet Ben Bella before giving an answer. Behja and I felt that she had acted smartly; we were only too aware of the obstacles to the marriage.

Zohra had courage and could be tough, if sometimes rash and unwise. She was also ambitious, held back by what she considered potent defects: namely, that she had been born and brought up in France, that her mother was French, and that she didn't speak or understand Arabic. She sought authenticity—to be regarded as a true-blue Algerian. What better way than through marriage to one of the country's legendary heroes? Hadj-Smaine's proposal surpassed her wildest dreams. It would eradicate forever any stigma of the outsider.

Zohra had never met the former president. In fact, she had been part of an opposition movement during his years in office. It was Zohra who had posed as the wife of opposition leader Mohamed Boudiaf in order to enable his real wife to sneak out of a hospital in Algiers, where she was being kept under guard, and leave the country. Quickly identified as the stand-in, Zohra was arrested and held for several days in a villa known for doubling as a torture chamber for adversaries of the Ben Bella regime. She recounted her experience with horror: while she herself had not been tortured, the screams of other inmates had pierced the walls of her cell throughout the night.

In addition, this man was some thirty years her senior. And how could a young, modern Algerian woman be expected to accept a proposal without even a formulaic face-to-face with a future husband?

It was agreed they would rendezvous at the prison residence, an address hidden from the public. Government security agents picked her up at her parents' home. They enclosed her behind thick black curtains in the back seat and, as if that was not enough, blindfolded her. She had the feeling it took hours to reach their destination, although she later learned that the building was located in the suburbs of Algiers.

Ben Bella was waiting for her. He opened the door as she approached. "It was love at first sight," she gushed to Behja and me.

Arrangements for the wedding moved forward without delay. However, a few days before the ceremony, President Boumediene ordered Zohra's father to come to his office at the Presidential Palace; this was the man who had overthrown his future son-in-law six years back. Also, it has to be said that Boumediene knew Zohra. She had been introduced to him earlier in the year, when he too had been looking to marry. As Zohra told it, it was not an engaging encounter. Conversation was halting and, when he moved to approach her, she stiffened and withdrew. There was no second meeting.

Mr. Sellami was escorted to the palace, where he was received alone by the all-powerful leader. Boumediene spoke of Zohra as one would of a friend or relative. He implored her father to refuse to permit his daughter to wed the ex-president. His clincher: "Don't you realize he is my enemy?"

Mr. Sellami was a small, wiry man with a bony face and a thin, arched nose. Boumediene must have towered over him. Following independence, he had returned to Algeria from France with his wife and three children: Zohra (the eldest), Said, and Farouk. In Paris, he had had a fruit-and-vegetable cart on the street; Mrs. Sellami worked in a laundry, while Zohra had a job as a salesgirl in a working-class department store. Mr. Sellami, who was barely literate, spoke often of his militant activities in the Fédération de France of the National Liberation Front, collecting and transporting money and arms for the Algerian cause during the war for independence.

Zohra and I were waiting for her father when he returned from his meeting with Boumediene. Visibly moved, he repeated word for word their exchange. "My daughter is a free woman," he had told the president. "I have always put my trust in her. When we lived in Paris, she was the only member of my family in whom I confided. She knew all about my militant activities, and I sometimes included her directly. On mission, she did her duty with courage. I cannot tell her who to marry. It's her decision."

He was ushered out.

The wedding took place in the little Sellami house, halfway up the winding rue Slimane Bedrani in the center of Algiers—a wedding with few guests, and no groom. It was early afternoon. Zohra was dressed in an elaborate, floor-length white lace dress. Gold bracelets lined her arms. Behja, who had borrowed the wedding gown and accessories from her mother and sisters, placed a diadem on Zohra's head. Her makeup emphasized her dark eyes and fine, clear skin: she was ravishing and elated. She repeated her vows, listened to the ritual prayers, and signed some papers that Hadj-Smaine whisked away. Then we danced, *youyoued*, and celebrated into the night.

A few days later, Zohra Sellami Ben Bella was driven—blind-folded again—to her husband's residence, where she remained for three weeks. As she was not a prisoner and could not be permanently confined, arrangements were made for her to come back to Algiers to spend a week at her parents' home, after which she returned to her husband for another three weeks, and so on.

Except for Behja and I, Zohra's friends withdrew from her, or looked the other way when she appeared. When she came to town to stay with her parents, she would call us. We visited with her, took her shopping, tried to enliven her stay. We updated her on what was going on in our lives. I kept her informed about Eldridge and the Panthers. She knew they could use both political and financial help, and spoke to Ben Bella. On one of her visits, she handed me a slip of paper that she had hidden in her panties before leaving their building. Written on it was the name and phone number of Ben Bella's lawyer in Paris: Madeleine Lafue-Véron.

On my next trip to Paris, I called Lafue-Véron. When I told her who had given me her number, she invited me to her apartment in Neuilly, an elegant residential neighborhood of Paris, close to the Bois de Boulogne. I was able to give her news of her client and of Zohra, whom she had not met and knew little about. She told me she had made several requests for authorization to visit Ben Bella in prison, to no effect. I promised I would stay in touch with her. I realized she was the pivot through which activists in France remained in touch and acted on Ben Bella's behalf, including with certain African leaders.

Zohra's routine continued until Boumediene died in 1978. Ben Bella was released from prison and placed under house arrest in M'Sila, the oasis town where Zohra's father had been born. There they remained until 1980 when the ex-president, after fifteen years of incarceration, regained his freedom of movement.

Moving On

Late one afternoon in 1972, as I was working at home in Algiers, there was a knock at the door. I opened to two men flashing official-looking ID. They told me to follow them to their car; they then drove me to the Ministry of Defense. For what purpose, they wouldn't say. I was aware that the Ministry was, among other things, the headquarters of the Sécurité Militaire (SM)—the political police, a powerful, all-invasive organ of the Algerian establishment. As the car sped along the upper boulevards, I remember noting that we were in the twilight zone, after hours.

I was led to an office without a window and seated in front of a desk to wait. I must have stayed put for two hours. Then, suddenly, the room was invaded by four men acting bullish and talking loudly. The first to enter, a chunky man with deep-set eyes and reddish hair and complexion, dressed in a well-pressed khaki uniform, was the lead interrogator. When he took off his military visor hat and laid it on the desk topside down I was able to read the inside label. His name was Ghaouti.[1]

I had been seated there long enough to figure out that the office was not a working office, but a room wired for recording. When the questions started—Who do you frequent? Who do they frequent? When were you last at so-and-so's?—I stopped him. I was frightened but, since I couldn't figure out where the interrogation was leading, I made a quick forward decision to halt it. "You don't need me to answer those questions. You must know the answers," I said.

Ghaouti laughed, then came out with it: "We want you to continue frequenting Zohra Sellami and report to us on her activities. If not, you'll be on the next plane out of Algeria." Once he'd let the monster out of the bag, he stood up, shook my hand, and told me his office would be in touch. The others filed out behind him. The play had come to its end. I was exhausted, troubled, and sad. The evening's message was clear: I was not free.

It was late by then and a driver took me home. There I contacted Mohamed Rezzoug, my upstairs neighbor and good friend, for advice. Mo was a leading functionary and knew most people worth knowing. He had that, for me, crucial quality—courage in the face of authority. Together we drafted a letter to Captain Ghaouti in which I stated my refusal to be an informer and said that, if forced to do so, I would prefer to leave the country. The next day Mo took the letter to Minister of Tourism Abdelaziz Maoui, who in the liberation war had been above the men running Sécurité Militaire now. He figured that would put an end to my travails.

I realized that I would have to stop seeing Zohra if I wanted to save my skin inside Algeria. After Maoui's intervention, to continue our meetings would be considered provocation. When she next called me, I told her I would not be able to meet her. I said it simply: "Zohra, I can't meet you, I'm sorry." I uttered a soft goodbye. I knew she would understand my refusal without belaboring the details. I was right. I never saw her again.

That same week, I received a phone call from an SM agent informing me that Zohra was in Algiers. I replied that I would not be meeting her. "Why not?" he asked.

"Because I don't intend to, that's all."

A day or two later, an agent arrived at my apartment with a tape recorder and the same question:

"Will you contact Madame Ben Bella?"

"No, I will not." He turned off his machine and left.

Several weeks went by and there they were again, the two agents, back at my door to take me to SM headquarters. The man waiting for me was the one who had sat closest to Ghaouti at our initial meeting. I can still see his face: oval and smooth, a bald egg, with large blue eyes.

He attacked me with fury, his face screwed up, just short of spitting at me: "You told her we contacted you and she complained to her husband. He said we're hassling his wife's friends! You'll pay for this."

He stalked out and slammed the door. When he came back he was waving a piece of paper that he handed over for my signature. It informed me that I had eight days to clear out of Algeria. There was no alternative. I signed.

On leaving I went directly to see my friend and former boss, Mohamed Benyahia, and told him my troubles. He made a phone call and reported that I would no longer be harassed. I relaxed. For a little over a year I was left in peace.

I later learned that Behja had also received a knock on her door. She was vulnerable—from a cop's standpoint—because she was living with an agricultural engineer of French nationality, René-Paul Traversac. She had just given birth to their daughter, Samia. Threats to deport René-Paul were intimidating, but Behja was Algerian, from a well-known family connected to the upper hierarchy.

Panther Finances

On leaving for France that July, I was determined to garner support for the Algiers group, to explain the Split, and to find funds. For a start, Carole Roussopoulos arranged for me to meet the filmmaker Jean-Luc Godard, her Swiss compatriot and long-time friend, who had introduced her to the Portapak. When I finished explaining the underlying causes of the Split, he raised his head stiffly, looked up and beyond me, and said: "What do you want from Godard?" The use of the third person put me off. I barely managed a reply: "Your support, your help." He dismissed me, turning his back.

Ellen Wright, Richard Wright's widow, a literary agent in Paris, made an appointment for me with her friend Simone de Beauvoir. I spent a lovely afternoon drinking tea with *la grande dame* in the living room of her art-deco apartment across the way from the Montparnasse cemetery. She was wearing a two-piece outfit of gray and cerulean blue, stockings, and solid shoes. On her head was a smallish gray kerchief, tied behind her ears. I found her attractive: she had very fine features, but her body was stiff. I spoke and she listened. At the end, she claimed that she was far removed from the matters I described, that she would have to consult with Jean-Paul Sartre. Would I call back? "Sartre," she told me a few days later, "is unwilling to support one group over the other."

Mokhtar's friends, Marque and Marcel Moiraud, organized an evening in their home with a group of committed political colleagues to listen to a French jazz singer, Colette Magny, where I made a pitch. Colette stated frankly that she favored Huey's side. The others were more receptive to my arguments, but no funds were forthcoming.

I had the feeling that Eldridge was being judged responsible for the Split—that he was too powerful a personality, which was unsettling for many. The facts didn't count as much as precon-ceptions and images. Deception also played its part. The Panthers had ignited groups around the world; their courage was infectious. They were emulated in England, in South Africa, in Australia, even in Israel. They were not designed to fail.

Jérôme Savary, whom I had known since he was a child—the irrepressible director of the Grand Magic Circus, France's first post–World War II attempt at musical comedy, and later director of the Théâtre National de Chaillot and the Opéra-Comique—agreed without hesitation to do a show dedicated to the Algiers Panthers and hand over the evening's proceeds, on condition that his crew of artistes agreed. They did, and I collected roughly $1,000 in francs after the performance.

While in Paris, I called the lawyer Lafue-Véron again. She invited me back to her apartment and asked whether I would be willing to meet Michalis Raptis, better known as Michel Pablo. "Of course I would!"

Former leader of the Fourth International, the Trotskyist organization that broke with the Comintern or Third International in 1939, Pablo—a Greek who had been deported from his own country before World War II and moved to Paris—was a controversial personality. As secretary of the Fourth International from 1948 to 1960, he is both credited with its restructuring and survival following World War II, and demonized for its subsequent divisions and marginalization. In the 1950s he espoused what was called entryism, or participation by Trotskyists in established socialist and trade union organizations, where they would quietly pull their weight as moles, one might say. In the late 1950s and 1960s he turned his energies to Third Worldism and joined, in particular, the Algerian struggle for independence behind the FLN. This was at a time when another splinter group of the Fourth International was backing Messali Hadj, the aging proponent of Algerian nationalism, who from his French outpost was waging a war to the death against the FLN both in France and Algeria. Messali had become the objective ally of France, the erstwhile colonial master.

Pablo's activism for the FLN is legendary: he was a hero. He invented a counterfeit-money scheme that was used on the international market to purchase arms for the Algerian Liberation Army. Arrested in the Netherlands on a charge of gun-running, he was convicted and spent over a year in jail. Liberated in 1960, he proceeded to Morocco, where he mounted an arms factory for the freedom fighters with fellow Trotskyist militants and Algerian combatants. After independence, he became a special advisor to President Ben Bella fostering *autogestion* (agricultural and industrial self-management), a system similar to the state planning introduced in Yugoslavia and Cuba. With the 1965 coup d'état he was gone from Algeria.

Pablo was waiting for me at the Café Cluny, on the corner of boulevard Saint-Michel and boulevard Saint-Germain. I recognized him under his fedora and headed for his table towards the back of the café's outdoor terrace.

He was curious to know how the Panthers had arrived in Algiers. "What kind of people are they? Their backgrounds? Who is Cleaver and what was the Split about?" We talked about the hijacking. Then came the sixty-four-dollar question: what was their future?

I explained that Ben Bella had suggested I contact his lawyer because, after the hijacking money was returned to the airlines, their situation had become increasingly precarious. They required air to breathe—and financing.

I had no idea where this contact would lead. When Mokhtar joined me in Paris, he too met with Pablo. Towards the end of the liberation war, Mokhtar had been stationed in the Signal Corps headquarters in Tunis and developed friendships with several militants associated with Pablo who were working for the Algerian provisional government. In the early days of independence, he took part in meetings with a group of progressives held in a quiet downtown café for discussions of government policy, in-depth criticism, and planning. Pablo had led those sessions. He remembered Mokhtar and was delighted to see him again. They talked at length on several occasions, reminiscing about people and events.

Hijackers, Again

In Detroit, a group of African Americans, each with their own charged personal history, had heard the story of Roger and Cathy's exploit. They had hooked up and together were seeking a way out of their dilemmas. Two of the men were prison escapees; one had been convicted of murder. The third was a deserter from the US army. With them were two women and three toddlers. They had been holed up in Detroit long enough to know there was no freedom for them, there or anywhere else in the United States. Adopting false identities and living on the run was not a solution, neither for them nor for their children. They would have to move on—out of the country. When they learned that an African American and his companion had hijacked a plane, received $500,000 in ransom for depositing the passengers, then obliged the pilot to fly them to Algiers where they were granted political asylum, they began laying plans. That, shortly after, the ransom had been returned to the airlines by the Algerian government escaped their notice.

The leader of the group was George Wright, the man convicted for the killing of a gas-station attendant in New Jersey in 1962 that had netted $70. Wright escaped from prison in 1970 with future co-hijacker George Brown, who was serving a three-to-five-year sentence for armed robbery. With two other inmates, they quietly took leave of their New Jersey farm prison between bed checks.

Jean and Melvin McNair grew up in North Carolina, where they met as students at Winston-Salem University and married. When Melvin enlisted and was stationed in Germany, Jean followed with their newborn son. Subjected to the army's brand of racism, administered by white officers mostly from the South, Melvin reacted. On learning that he was scheduled to leave for Vietnam, he revolted and walked out of the army. "No Vietnamese ever called me nigger," he told the court during his extradition trial in Paris in 1975.

Joyce Tillerson, the second woman and mother in the group, was a friend of the McNairs. The group developed a common spiritual identity and practiced various rituals—which Eldridge labeled "voodoo"—inspired by their vision of Africa. A return to their "homeland" was to be their blessing.

The hijacking of Delta Air Lines flight 841 from Detroit to Miami was prepared methodically. Wright boarded the plane dressed in the black garb of a Catholic priest. The Bible he held firmly in his hands had been hollowed out to encase a pistol. While Wright took control of the pilots, the other two men held the passengers at bay with revolvers that had been buried in the kids' clothing. They procured a million-dollar ransom in Miami, then flew to Boston to take on a navigator for the overseas leg of the trip.

The plane landed successfully in Algiers on August 1, 1972, but the scenario that followed differed from the earlier one involving Roger and Cathy. The Algerian authorities closed the airport and handled things alone. The Panthers were informed and made it to the airport, but were not allowed contact with the hijackers. On the road back to the city, the Panthers tried to approach the bus transporting the hijackers to warn them to keep the money in their possession. The plane began its return journey to the US the night of its arrival in Algeria; the Panthers feared that the money would take the same route. Four days later the group was dropped off at the Embassy.

While Algeria was avowedly Third World and an outspoken critic of the colonialist and imperialist West, it was in no way a "rogue" state. The authorities wanted it to be known that anyone entertaining thoughts of skyjack aimed at their country should understand that the Algerian government was not their accomplice, even if it judged the hijackers to be victims of an unjust society and was willing to guarantee their personal safety by granting asylum.

In Limbo

Obsessed by the million-dollar bounty that was escaping their hands, the Algiers Panthers and the hijackers pondered over what action to undertake, what pressure to apply. They were "vibrating to the overtones of dollar bills. They lost all proportion or any sense thereof," Eldridge later commented. When they started drafting a letter of grievance to be made public, DC, the Panthers' former top military man, warned his colleagues that they were heading for self-destruction: "I told them they was crazy. The government is not going to risk the future of their country for a handful of niggas and a million dollars . . . They was gonna be in trouble."[2]

And trouble there was. They drafted an open letter to President Boumediene: "Those who deprive us of this finance are depriving us of our freedom . . . What we are asking is that the Algerian government not fight the battles of the American government for the ruling circles that are oppressing the whole of the American people . . . Let it not be said that Algeria has turned its back on the struggle of the Afro-American people." The letter was deposited at the presidential palace and delivered to the international press.

On August 10, the Algerian police raided the Panther villa in El Biar and confiscated their weapons. Telephone and telex communications were cut. Guards stationed at the entrance to the villa let no one in or out. The siege lasted until the following evening. Then silence: nothing until August 16, when Eldridge was summoned to a meeting with the head of state security, Salah Hidjeb. The open letter to Boumediene had the effect of a bomb. How could they openly reproach their benefactors with betraying them? Attempt to shame Boumediene into releasing the hijack money to them?

Hidjeb's comments and the tone of the discussion with the Panthers—as Cleaver's notes of the interview reveal—indicate that the Algerians had decided to let the Panthers know who was boss; but, at the same time, to gloss over the events and let the matter drop. In response, Pete O'Neal, who was also in the room, offered to leave the country, if the Algerian authorities financed their departure. Hidjeb was clearly startled, but made no comment.

He was also told that, in two days, the Panthers intended to celebrate August 18 as International Day of Solidarity with the Afro-American People. Invitations and press releases had already been issued. Hidjeb agreed to have the telephone and telex connections restored in time. I was in Paris, but Eldridge was able to get through to me by phone to complain that, despite Hidjeb's promises, plainclothes policemen were stationed at the gate in front of the Embassy and were turning away the journalists, diplomats and representatives of liberation movements arriving for the solidarity event.

That guard was lifted the following day, the same day *El Moudjahid* published the text of a message from the hitherto unheard-of Algerian Committee for African-American Solidarity, reiterating its "indefatigable support for the just cause of oppressed peoples, saluting the combat of the Afro-American people and assuring them of our support and solidarity." Rich examples of official double-talk.

Eldridge's frantic calls from Algiers had put me on edge. I came up with an idea: he could commit to passing the money on to Palestinian freedom fighters, thus injecting a new element, via organizations closer emotionally to the Algerian side, into the scenario. I prepared a press release in his name, typed it, and took it to the French morning daily *Libération*, where it was published the following day. I had not consulted Eldridge. There was no way I would have announced my plan in an open telephone conversation between Paris and Algiers. I did ask Michel Pablo for advice; he approved, but thought there was little chance of success. In Algiers, Eldridge pledged to "donate half of it, $500,000, to the Palestinian people" and prepared a written statement to that effect, which was never made public. The money returned to the airlines as soon as arrangements were finalized.

The publicized letter to Boumediene was a gaffe that illustrated how little the Panthers understood Third World politics. They refused to acknowledge the power relationship between themselves and the Algerian political hierarchy. Cleaver and his companions were thousands of miles from home in a country they had idolized from afar. Their knowledge of Algeria was based on images from the Algerian war of independence, on Pontecorvo's film *The Battle of Algiers*, on Frantz Fanon's writings and Malcolm X's Americanized brand of Islam. In Algiers they never ventured beyond the city. Even with their increasing knowledge of French, they didn't read the press or listen to the local radio. Except for women friends, they knew few Algerians and never visited Algerian homes. They had no perspective on the colonial past in Algeria, the ravages of the war, or the profound under-development that the regime was attempting to tackle. They saw themselves as free agents, able to deploy the powers of protest and the media as they wished. Some among them went so far as to propose organizing a protest march in front of President Boumediene's offices. Cleaver had to remind them that this was Algiers, "not Harlem." They had no serious sense of their hosts, of their politics or their reservations, and they underestimated them.

The Algerians, for their part, had never known any Americans, let alone Black Americans. They were at a loss as to how to deal with them. They were suspicious of them and in awe of their life-style, their prowess and efficiency. They represented the modern world. When the Panthers arrived, Algeria was a leading light in the Third World, active in international politics and the non-aligned group of nations. They were hosting and training liberation move-ments from Latin America, Africa and Asia. There was too much at stake for them to be pushed around by American exiles, whatever their plight. And they could not allow international hijackers to turn them into a miscreant nation that failed to abide by the rules.

Since no further punitive action was taken, I can only assume that the Algerian authorities were not ready to throw to the wolves the representatives of a tortured, hunted minority, citizens of the world power that was at war in the Third World against a major Algerian ally, Vietnam.

There were certainly members of the Algerian political elite who sought to cement relations with the United States, at the expense of the Panthers or anyone else. Some time later I learned that on a trip to Hanoi, Minister of Foreign Affairs Abdelaziz Bouteflika (now president of Algeria) had requested the government of North Vietnam to hand over its American prisoners of war, so that he personally might release them to the American government. The Vietnamese refused his offer in the most courteous diplomatic language.

By a trick of fate, a stack of American passports was lifted off a desk in a Parisian travel agency as they awaited visas for their owners' trips to foreign parts. The young African American who walked out the door with those documents understood that he was in possession of a pot of gold. He was not a Panther, but he was certainly ennobled with revolutionary clairvoyance: he decided to deliver the passports into the hungry hands of Eldridge Cleaver in Algiers.

This windfall took place at a time when Eldridge was personally involved in the planning and organization of an international air-piracy project with members of the German Red Army Faction (RAF), also known as the Baader-Meinhof Group. The plan was for a small unit of highly motivated individuals representing the RAF, Palestinian freedom fighters, and the Panthers (i.e., Eldridge) to hijack a passenger plane that would circle Europe's skies. While in the air they would demand the liberation of American, Palestinian, and German political prisoners, notably members of the Baader-Meinhof Group, in exchange for the lives of the passengers and crew.

A Wedding and Its Consequences

During the latter half of 1972, the representative of the Red Army Faction moved in and out of Algiers with ease and frequency. We called her Ann. She was light-skinned, blondish, and slim. She always wore jeans and moved rapidly, sure of herself, not easily rattled.

At that time, airports were beefing up security for the express purpose of putting an end to hijacking. Metal detectors were already in place at major US airports and were being installed worldwide, though not yet at Algiers's Dar El Beïda. Ann visited airports in and around Africa, verifying their state of preparedness. She located a number of places where major international airlines—particularly Lufthansa—dropped off and picked up passengers, airports where security equipment had not been installed and controls were lax, among them Casablanca, Morocco. Plans for a sophisticated hijacking operation were moving forward when the pile of US passports landed in Algiers.

Like airports, passports were not foolproof. With the right equipment and some degree of expertise, photos could be replaced, entry and exit stamps copied and applied. Respecting the official guidelines for US passports, the hijackers and Panthers who lacked documentation had their photos taken. We fitted the identifying data of the stolen passports as closely as possible to the characteristics of those who would be using them, although that was of little consequence: it was rare for border-control agents to match American passport photos with their data as to height, hair, and eye color, or to check the age of their bearers. The fact that the original passport holders were white would be obscured once the new photos were in place.

Before I left Algiers for Europe, Eldridge gave me a German telephone number to memorize. I stowed the passports and photos in an over-the-shoulder bag that I held close to my body, and flew to Paris. At the Gare de l'Est, I boarded a late morning train to Frankfurt, feeling comfortable with my mission. But as the train crossed into Germany and uniformed officials came on board, I stiffened. I hadn't realized that the European Union's open borders for products and individuals throughout the Western European countries had not eliminated border controls between France and Germany. A German officer opened the door to my compartment and called for everyone's ID. I handed over my American passport. It was returned without comment. My innards relaxed.

In Frankfurt, I called the memorized phone number and was given an address. The taxi dropped me off in a bourgeois section of the city in front of what looked to be a large, comfortable one-family home. The man who answered the door had been expecting me. He showed me to a bedroom on the third floor, where I spent the night; I handed over the documents and photos. I told him I had a message for our contact Ann. Was she available?

That night food was laid out in the ground-floor kitchen. Several young people were milling about and acknowledged me, but there was no spontaneous conversation. After breakfast the next morning, my host informed me that the passports would be ready at the end of the day and that Ann would meet me in the afternoon at a coffeehouse in downtown Frankfurt.

I arrived at the café early and watched the woman coming toward me with awe. This was not the blue-jeaned hippy I'd met in Algiers. Ann's eyes were edged in greenish mascara, her hair blonder and styled. A neat pillbox hat sat squarely on her head. She wore heels, stockings, and a well-tailored navy-blue suit. When I told her there was something Marlene Dietrich about her, she laughed and intimated there might be some connection.

I had a message for Ann from Eldridge: he was pulling out of the RAF hijacking operation, and requested that the comrades not include Algeria's airports in their plans. Ann laughed shortly and snapped, "Tell him not to worry, we won't use his Boumediene's country for the hijacking." She emphasized the *his*. We talked of other things, kissed, and parted.

Later that evening the passports were returned to me. I checked them out and felt that they would pass inspection at border controls. The photos were impressed with something resembling the US government seal and imprint. The following morning I took the train to Paris, then traveled on to Algiers by plane.

We soon realized, however, that we were missing a vital element for the new passports: an entry stamp into Algeria. How do you leave a country if you haven't been processed in with a stamp in your passport? Eldridge contacted the German group, and Ann arrived in short order with the proper utensil. She sat at the worktable in my apartment and applied the stamp to the passports as Eldridge, Mokhtar, and I stood around admiring the deftness of her hands. With Eldridge she was cool, nothing amiss, despite his withdrawal from the hijacking project.

I never saw Ann again. For months afterward, I waited expectantly for that hijacking to be announced in large print. But nothing happened.

Five years later, on October 13, 1977, a Lufthansa passenger jet was hijacked on its flight from an island in the Mediterranean—Majorca, Spain—to Frankfurt by four Palestinians, two women and two men: Wabil Harb, Hind Alameh, Zohair Akache, and Suhaila Sayeh. The air pirates demanded the release of "our comrades in German prisons." Specifically, they sought the liberation of eleven RAF prisoners—Andreas Baader included—and two Palestinians being held in Germany. The hijacking ended on the tarmac of the Mogadishu airport in Somalia, when a specially trained German commando stormed the plane. Three of the four hijackers were killed; Suhaila Sayeh survived. Five days later, on October 18, the RAF leaders Andreas Baader, Gudrun Ensslin, and Jan-Carl Raspe were found dead in their prison cells. Irmgard Möller was wounded but alive. The German authorities claimed that the group committed collective suicide. Irmgard Möller, who survived four stabs to her breast with a kitchen knife, stated that there was no suicide pact, that it was murder by a special commando. Other former RAF militants have maintained it was collective suicide.

With a broken organization in the United States and international support sliding fast, the International Panthers were close to stateless. The crackdown after their open letter to Boumediene highlighted the need for each one to envisage their own future. They squabbled: Who was to blame? Who was in charge?

Don Cox had resigned, and was living at Pointe Pescade along the coast with the newly arrived hijacker families. Eldridge turned official representation over to Pete O'Neal and moved out of the Embassy to a small, elegant apartment further down the hill toward the city. Kathleen and the children were shipped out to the United States, then to Europe. The first air pirates, Cathy and Roger, set up in my place until I returned from Paris in early September, after which they occupied a large downtown apartment with an extravagant view of the Mediterranean for which Eldridge had promised key money that he never paid. It was well situated for "turning tricks" when finances demanded.

The Panthers were still receiving their monthly stipend from the FLN liberation-movement office. But, to quote Eldridge, "the International Section had become a sinking ship." The time had come to think in terms of survival: how to stay alive and a few steps ahead of US law enforcement. To remain in Algeria was a solution they summarily rejected. I was convinced that life in Algeria could have been made viable, even long-term. Their lack of language fluency could have been compensated by their technical skills and capacity for work. They were in no mind, however, to negotiate their future with functionaries they now considered enemies.

Connie Matthews and Michael "Cetewayo" Tabor were the first to pull out of Algiers. They headed for Zambia, the former British colony of Northern Rhodesia. Cetewayo, a native of Harlem, was both streetwise and profound. He had a strong, deep voice that resonated like a melodious boombox. His pamphlet "Capitalism Plus Dope Equals Genocide," essential BPP literature, developed from his own drama as a heroin addict:

> Capitalist exploitation and racial oppression are the main contributing factors to drug addiction in regard to Black people . . . The government is totally incapable of addressing itself to the true causes of drug addiction for to do so would necessitate effecting a radical transformation of this society.[3]

That Cetewayo became a leading journalist in Zambia was no surprise. The last time I spoke with him by telephone from New York, he was in broadcasting, managing several radio and news programs. He died in 2010 in exile.

Connie Matthews was petite and fine-boned; her high cheekbones led smoothly to a neat, tapered chin. She was also lovely to listen to, her British accent peppered with Panther "down" talk.

She was quick-witted, an educated dynamo. Originally from Jamaica, Connie had lived in Europe for much of her adult life, studying in London and Vienna where she obtained a master's degree in psychology, and working for UNESCO before joining the Panthers full-time. Prior to her Panther connection, she had not set foot in the United States. Connie and Cet's marriage did not survive the strains of their new circumstances. Still the militant, she returned to Jamaica, where she died of cancer in 1993.

Pete and Charlotte O'Neal and their little boy flew to Cairo, then on to Tanzania, where they had friends. They settled in the northern part of the country, near Arusha. They not only have made a life for themselves but transformed the lives of their neighbors. Pete and Charlotte hail from Kansas City, where Pete, a small-time criminal and pimp, was transformed by the Black Panthers. He created and animated a strong local party until his arrest on trumped-up gun charges that would have put him in prison for several years. He and Charlotte slipped out of the US with false documents and joined Cleaver in Algiers.

They are now farmers in the African bush, where they have raised and educated their own three children as well as a slew of others from the surrounding tribes. They have created schools, health centers, and an exchange program for young African Americans. Charlotte and the children have all been back to the US. As for Pete, despite the attempts of sympathetic politicians, he has not been granted a pardon: it would require him to apologize for a crime that never took place, something he refuses to do.

James "Akili" Patterson, his wife Gwen, and their daughter, Tania, had arrived in Algiers from Havana. To reach Cuba from the United States they had hijacked a plane. The couple suffered badly in exile. After Eldridge expelled Akili from the BPP, he took off for Liberia, where rumor had it he became a successful businessman. Gwen was left to become a nanny for the Panther children in Algiers. She sank slowly into depression. I arranged for her to be hospitalized. In desperation, Kathleen asked Slimane Hoffman to have her repatriated. He furnished Gwen with a ticket to the States.

New York Panthers Larry Mack and Sekou Odinga slipped back into the US. Sekou lived and organized underground for years before his arrest following the Brink's robbery of October 1981, in which two police officers and a Brink's guard were killed. After more than thirty years in prison, he was released in November 2014.

The Detroit hijackers stayed in Algeria for another eight months before entering France by ship in 1973. They were aided by an organization of French left-wing intellectuals headed by the Egyptian Henri Curiel, who was himself assassinated in 1978 in Paris by two unidentified men—presumed to have been hired by white South African fascists, and given the go-ahead by the militia of the ruling Gaullist party.

A recent documentary by Maia Wechsler, *Melvin and Jean: An American Story*, follows the saga of the McNairs (two members of the second group of hijackers who became upstanding citizens of France), in a vivid, moving presentation in which I play a brief role. Jean McNair died in 2014. The California hijackers, Roger and Cathy, remained in their downtown apartment in Algiers for a year and a half, until January 1974, when they left for Europe, settling in Paris. I helped prepare their exit through Geneva, with Cathy wearing my clothes and green leather boots for the trip. As a couple, they soon fell apart. Roger eventually returned to the United States. Cathy has disappeared without a trace.

Don Cox left for the States and a clandestine existence, until his close-up view of post-Panther reality convinced him that no rise in revolutionary fervor and organization was on the cards for some time to come. He returned to Algeria in early 1974 and lived and worked there for four more years as an industrial photographer, heading the photo lab of the Société Nationale de Sidérurgie, the national ironworks. DC had been the field marshal of the BPP before leaving for Algiers. His booklet on military preparedness became a standard BPP text, used throughout the organization to build an underground network capable of launching direct action. Revolutionary groups elsewhere, including in Africa, have sought his text and used its guidelines.

DC was a beautiful man, handsome, genuine, giving. We maintained contact and mutual support until his death in France in 2011. When he left Algeria for France in 1977, I introduced him to Bernard Stasi, the mayor of Épernay, who intervened on his behalf for residence papers. DC had grown up on a farm in Missouri and returned to farming again in southwestern France, raising aromatic plants for the perfume industry. He was my dearest friend in the Panther organization and is sorely missed.

The fact that no one was put on a plane and ejected from Algeria, that even following the events involving the second planeload of hijackers, no one was told to leave the country, is proof that the Panthers were not "thrown out," as numerous writers have claimed. They all left of their own accord. Eldridge, DC, and all the hijackers stayed on in Algiers for varying periods of time. It is understandable that for some of the departing members of the International Section, the events that they lived through following their open letter to Boumediene constituted a death knell. I am affirming, however, that no one was deported.

Among the passports I brought back from Frankfurt, there was one for Eldridge. He looked it over, fondled it, and then, looking me straight in the face, said slowly: "I'm going to use it, Elaine. I'm going to France."

To stay on in Algeria, he reasoned, was a dead end. The International Section of the BPP had become deflated. The Panthers in the States were dying, individually and as an organization. The Split had precipitated the end. Eldridge longed to return to an environment that he could deal with, on terms he understood better than those of a semi-dictatorship he found difficulty navigating. He craved something of the life he had led back in California. It wasn't yet apparent, perhaps not even to him, but he had begun the process of resigning from the left.

Kathleen took their children to the States to be cared for, then flew to Europe in the hope of finding a country willing to offer refuge to her family. She traveled to Scandinavia and to Switzerland, but Eldridge had already decided he would try his luck in France.

In December 1972, I went to Paris to make the arrangements. Michel Pablo, our Trotskyist contact, helped me lay plans. We decided that Eldridge would be less exposed traveling from Tunisia. Paul Roussopoulos volunteered to drive him from Algiers to the oasis in Tozeur, where he and his wife Carole owned a house. Border controls would be lax there; they could spend the night in that otherworldly setting of date palms and desert and then drive to Tunis.

To fly into Switzerland from Tunis would be the least risky. Pablo gave me the phone number of a "passer" who could rendezvous with Eldridge at the airport in Geneva. He would drive him into France, skirting the official frontier posts. I charged a good and trustworthy friend, Andréa Thibault, with the task of contacting the passer personally and setting up the signals for his intervention. She left for Geneva and came back the next day with the information we required.

Yves Antoine, a Parisian architect friend, agreed to drive me to Besançon, a small city in eastern France close to the Swiss border, where the passer would drop Eldridge and we would retrieve him. I arranged with my friends Nicole and Pierre Chapo to house him on arrival at their isolated ranch house outside of Gordes, a small hilltop town in southern France. That was as far ahead as I could see and manage at the time.

When everything was wrapped up, Pablo handed me a classy British passport with a photo of a Black man who could have been a younger Eldridge. It was brand-new, "clean," and safer than the stolen, doctored American passport. We had only to add the Algerian entry stamp and he would be on his way.

To avoid making telephone contact, I traveled to Gordes to put it to the Chapos in person.

"*C'est bon*," they said. "There's always someone here."

"He'll make an engaging houseguest," I said.

On December 21, I flew back to Algiers from Marseille. I found Eldridge getting ready, outfitting himself, and making his farewells to those he was close to. But when he asked for the keys to my apartment "in order to say goodbye to someone," I flipped. That "someone" was a veiled lady who lived on one of the upper floors. Eldridge often took my keys during the day. He said my apartment was an oasis of peace, far from the noise and agitation of the Embassy. I had imagined him there reading, writing at the table, dozing off. That he had forged an intimate connection with a lady in the next stairwell was mind-blowing. He told me everything had started one day as he parked my car behind the building, while the mysterious lady was on her back balcony hanging the laundry out to dry. This was a woman permanently closeted in her apartment, who only ventured outside when accompanied by a male member of her family. But, somehow, Eldridge had been secretly rendezvousing with her for months. I learned to put nothing past him, as would be clear to all the world as his life wound on.

He said goodbye to his special people, Malika included, whom he also saw at my apartment. They were no longer lovers: he was by then involved with another charming Algerian woman, whom I shall call B. He insisted on telling me how proud he was of Malika. She was working in a trade union, organizing, speaking in public; she had become a militant for workers' rights. He described the maturing Malika as a father might, as the man who had formed her, taught her the ropes, and sent her on her way.

Two days before Eldridge was due to leave, a friend I had been close to since my first days in Algiers, Francine Serfati, asked me whether it was true that Cleaver was going to France. "What did you say?" I stammered, trying to hold my face steady. I looked straight at her and replied that it was totally untrue, false, no way. I was overcome by the carelessness of the Panthers, their inability to keep their information to themselves. "If you say so," she muttered.

Paul and Eldridge left Algiers early on New Year's Day, 1973. Mokhtar and I had been drinking and stomping at a New Year's party and had rolled home at three or four in the morning. I somehow extracted myself from the warmth of our bed and at 6 a.m. drove to the Panther Embassy to say adieu.

I couldn't believe what I saw. Eldridge was transformed, his big frame clothed in a heavy, long, dark-gray chesterfield. His face was clean-shaven and he was wearing a homburg, a hat I hadn't seen on anybody in years. I couldn't help wondering if it would attract more attention to him than he needed. One of his hands firmly gripped a rolled black umbrella, à la Anthony Eden, the other an attaché case. He was sweating profusely despite the morning chill.

He hugged me. I said "*À bientôt*," went back to Mokhtar's bed and cried uncontrollably. An era of my life was ending.

On January 2, I left for Paris. In the early afternoon of the January 5, I met Yves Antoine—driving a fairly comfortable black Peugeot—in front of his apartment building on the rue Saint-Romain in the sixth arrondissement. We took off for the 400-kilometer drive, four to five hours, nervous, anxious for Eldridge. He would have traveled through three national borders: Algeria–Tunisia, Tunisia–Switzerland, and Switzerland–France. At any one of them—the last two in particular—he was at risk of arrest and extradition to the US. Would he be waiting for us on the Grande Rue in the center of Besançon at seven o'clock?

On the dot of seven we drove up. There he was, alone, still sweating. He cracked a smile when he saw me, took off the homburg, threw it, the umbrella, and his suitcase into the trunk, and lunged into the front seat. I got in back. Antoine knew how to get us to Beaune and Lyon where we picked up the Autoroute du Soleil, the A7. Eldridge was silent for a long while. He was exhausted, slowly collecting himself. Antoine and I talked some, mainly about the road and traffic. "Gordes is five to six hours away," he muttered.

At some point, Eldridge came to and opened up, reliving his trip. The desert oasis at Tozeur was romantic "digs." The airport in Tunis was "horrible: everyone was staring at the big black dude in diplomatic gear." In Geneva, he was tongue-tied. Luckily, he didn't have to speak, just show his passport. The passer had been on time. He had walked out of the air terminal to his car, with Eldridge following at a short distance. They took the back roads and barely spoke. At one turn of the road, the man had pointed to an official frontier post in the distance. "They won't notice us," he had assured Eldridge.

Near Cavaillon, we turned onto the D900. From there I leaned forward from the back seat to direct us along the dark back roads, through the minute hamlets of Goult and Saint-Pantaléon to the plain below Gordes where the ranch house sat. The beams radiating from the Peugeot were the only lights to be seen anywhere. I knew those winding trails by heart. In years past, I had lived here off-and-on with Nicole and Pierre. Neither Antoine nor Eldridge said a word.

We arrived well after midnight. At the sound of our engine, the house lit up. Nicole came running out and threw her arms around us all. Eldridge looked stunned. I yelled: "We made it! Here's your boarder, Nicole!"

Antoine and I stayed at the ranch for several days, until there was nothing to do but leave Eldridge there. He seemed comfortable with Nicole and her sons Nicholas and Fidel; her husband, Pierre, was in Strasbourg on business. The ranch was not a ranch in the traditional sense, though it covered a nice plot of land. The only animals it sheltered were a large flock of geese that Pierre liked to conduct for walks around the property. It was an image he cultivated. He was an artist at heart, though he survived by making modern furniture with traditional techniques.

Nicole was close to fifty, a rather heavy woman, tall for the French, prematurely gray, with pale green eyes. She spoke a quirky, easy kind of English and had a great sense of humor, loud and quick on the uptake. A painter and sculptor, she announced she would do a bust of Eldridge.

Eldridge relaxed. He loved Nicole's fast, tasty food. We drove him around the area from Apt to Cavaillon to l'Isle-sur-la-Sorgue. He stood out, the only black man in sight, towering over everyone. He got used to mixing with people in the street and to being seen in public, and—surprise—no one recognized him.

I went back to Paris and then to Algiers. We hadn't figured out our next step.

Towards the end of January 1973, Eldridge wrote to say he was ready to move from Gordes, to Paris if possible. He had had enough of anonymity. He wanted to get back in action, move on. What could I arrange?

I returned to France and contacted my old architect friend Pierre Ristorcelli, who had a furnished one-bedroom apartment on the rue Saint-Jacques, in the Latin Quarter, that was unoccupied. He agreed to lend it to Eldridge.

As I prepared to leave for Gordes to oversee the transfer, sweet little B. arrived from Algiers. Where was Eldridge? When could she see him? She was desperate for news and eager to rendezvous with him. I borrowed a Beetle Volkswagen from my close friend Cynthia Horn and we took to the highway for the daylong journey. It rained all the way south and we ran out of gas a kilometer from a gas pump. We were on the toll highway, so I waited in the car while B. walked to the service station. We made it to the ranch house just as night fell. Eldridge was excited to see us; B. was ecstatic. She kept jumping up and down. The first thing I noticed on entering was the plaster bust that Nicole had sculpted of her guest. It sits today at the entrance to Fidel Chapo's art locale near Gordes, a wonderful likeness.

B. and I spent the weekend at the ranch. We decided it was best that Nicole, who was French, escort Eldridge to Paris rather than us, two non-resident foreigners. In any case, we had to return the borrowed car.

When Nicole and Eldridge left Gordes, they added a large container of Riesling and kilos of *choucroute* to the luggage, both of which Pierre Chapo had brought back from Strasbourg. As soon as they arrived at the apartment in Paris, Nicole set to work preparing the sausages, ham, bacon, spices, and condiments to add to the *choucroute*, and laid out a feast for all our friends, Eldridge's new benefactors.[4] We were proud of our coup—we all had a hand in landing him safely in France and now in Paris. Circling around a beaming Cleaver, we lifted our glasses and toasted: *Santé! Longue vie!*

Carole and Paul Roussopoulos introduced Eldridge to Jean Genet, the radical French dramaturge. At their first meeting, Genet listened to Eldridge praise "democratic France" in glowing terms, describing the country as "on a collision course with the United States." Genet reacted sharply, attacking him for being naïve: "Not only you're a child, you're 'white!'" he cried.[5] He went to work to darken Eldridge's view of French history: the wars, the atrocities, the injustices and racism of succeeding French administrations.

That prickly first encounter did not stop Genet from introducing Eldridge to Roland Dumas, a prominent French lawyer who, in the 1980s, would become minister of foreign affairs under François Mitterrand. Genet assured Eldridge that Dumas could handle any legal hassles he might face.

On April 5, 1973, Dumas and human rights lawyer Jean-Jacques de Félice addressed a petition to Pierre Messmer, head of the French government, requesting political asylum for Eldridge Cleaver. They backed it up with a supporting statement and an appeal signed by a range of French intellectuals, including de Beauvoir and Sartre. When the request was ignored by the French premier, Mitterrand, then the opposition leader, raised the case in the National Assembly. Minister of the Interior Raymond Marcellin replied that Cleaver "runs no particular risk in his present country of residence [Algeria] due to his political convictions or his ethnic origin." In other words, let him stay in Algeria.

Eldridge wasted no time contacting friends in Paris and making new ones. Old friends started arriving from the States. The social whirl he thrived on had begun, even though he was illegal and would remain so for another year.

Mokhtar had arrived in Paris to renew his university permits. We returned to Algiers together, stopping in Gordes to see the Chapos. The day of our departure, the air traffic controllers went on strike. We learned that some planes to foreign destinations were still taking to the air, so we went to the airport in Marseille. After going through passport control, we waited in the departure hall for several hours for the plane to Algiers. Suddenly my name was broadcast over the speaker system. I was beckoned to a small office, where a security agent informed me that I was ordered to leave France and not return. I was given papers to sign certifying that I had received official notification of the interdiction to enter French territory. No reason was given. Since I was a journalist, the agent asked whether it might be something I'd written. I knew better but didn't say so.

I returned to my classes at the School of Journalism. My liaison with Mokhtar was strong and consuming. We didn't miss a day.

Despite the interdiction, Mokhtar and I decided to spend the summer in Europe. I left first, confident that my American passport would not be scrutinized at Orly. The days of electronic examination and no-fly lists were still a long way in the future. I showed my passport to the official on duty, he stamped and returned it, and I walked through the gates into France.

I left my bag at the Chapos' apartment on boulevard de l'Hôpital and headed for Eldridge's place. As I got off the bus at the corner of the rue Saint-Jacques, I could see people milling about in the street and outside the Institut Sourd-Muet across the way from his building. When I looked up at the fifth-floor window, there he was, waving to me with one of those giant hands. The photographers and newsmen hanging out in front of the doorway let me through. Eldridge had been discovered. Anonymity was no more, and he was thrilled. I wondered how it had come about. I suspected that he had engineered it in order to move ahead, to push the politicos' buttons so that they would come to a decision on his request for asylum.

Any positive side to the press presence was short-lived, however, and did not lead to a decision to provide refugee status to the Cleavers. On the contrary, there was an element of danger that Eldridge could not ignore, since the police now knew where to find him. Everyone, including Roland Dumas, advised him to leave the rue Saint-Jacques for more discreet quarters. Once again the Chapos came to the rescue, with a studio at the Sèvres-Babylone intersection in the seventh arrondissement that had belonged to Pierre's parents. Eldridge left the rue Saint-Jacques late at night, after the press had retired to bed.

I saw Eldridge often that summer, and watched as he became involved with the wife of one of his backers and the girlfriend of one of his buddies. The latter paid no mind, but the former became so deranged as to attempt suicide. As I was leaving Paris, Eldridge handed me a small wrapped box and asked me to deliver it to Malika in Algiers. I would only learn its contents and significance forty-four years later, in 2017, when thanks to a grand stroke of luck I found myself once again in touch with lovely Malika. Inside lay a lock of her hair and what, coming from Eldridge, might be called a love letter, ending with the words "Right On."

Kathleen was still traveling around Europe. Eldridge was on his own, manufacturing a new life out of his old one and enjoying it. He had discarded responsibility for the members or the tribe—whatever it was that the International Section represented for him in its dying stages. "To each his own" was the new watchword. That included me, though we never said the words. I had given him what I could, the bounties of my twenty-something years in France and Algeria. I understood the day he left Algiers that the bonds we had tied would unravel. I could now see it happening.

What I didn't know was that one day I would be needing him.

Several years later, Eldridge claimed that he had survived in Algeria by dealing in passports and stolen cars: "My criminal education in East Los Angeles," he wrote in *Soul on Fire*, "helped us out significantly in North Africa. The first effort that paid off for us was trafficking in stolen passports and counterfeiting visas . . . with a unique portable process . . . Portable meant that we could change passports right at an airport locker room, even use the same document for different people traveling—just keep changing the pictures."[6] According to the same passage, the Panthers "used to run stolen cars from Europe . . . Cars we brought into Algeria found their way throughout the Third World."[7]

Such information has been reproduced by a number of serious writers and journalists researching the Panther experience in Algeria. I realize it comes directly from Eldridge—from the horse's mouth, so to speak. This information was published in *Soul on Fire*, the autobiography that Eldridge published in 1978 with an obscure American publisher, a book, I believe, that was intended to redress his image in order to gain status on what he termed the "soul circuit." Does anyone really believe that the International Section of the BPP was a mafia operation in a malefic country? Nothing could be further from the truth. The passports stolen in Paris by someone unknown to the BPP—which I took to Germany to be transformed—were used by the Panther contingent for one purpose: for themselves to travel outside Algeria. Even more incredible, he claims that "a couple of the American office types had slipped some passport blanks out of the embassy, and we were in business."[8] We didn't have the know-how to doctor passports and, as I've said, we had to bring Ann from Germany to Algiers to make those we had serviceable, by adding the Algerian arrival stamp. As for cars, the Panthers were in possession of a used van and a new minibus offered by their German support group—that's all. Nothing could be more far-fetched than the tale of a ring of Black American car thieves functioning between Europe and Algiers under the nose of a heavily policed regime, selling automobiles like cookies at a street fair.

Eldridge was once offered the chance to become a true mafioso in Algeria, and he turned it down. Contacted by an African American with a proposition to set up a relay station in Algeria for drugs from Latin America on their way to Europe, he warned the contact to stay clear of his country. He might later choose to forget how much he owed his North African benefactors for his safety, but at the time he was highly aware of his responsibility for the lives of several dozen women, men, and children.

At the end of December 1973, I left for Tunis to renew my Algerian visa. For years I had been without a residence permit. During the Panther days I had been able to go in and out of the country simply by contacting the FLN liberation-movement office, which also arranged for my departure and reception at the airport. Now that the Panthers were gone, it was time to get my status in order: reapply for a visa, then request a residence permit. I stayed with friends in Tunis and made an application at the Algerian consulate for the work visa I had received in the past. I contacted the consulate several times, but the authorization was not coming through. The consul, an old friend of Mokhtar's from the war years, received me; but without authorization from Algiers there was no way he would issue a visa.

A friend of my Tunis hosts offered to call Madame Burr, the personal assistant to Minister of Foreign Affairs Abdelaziz Bouteflika, and ask her to intervene. Madame Burr remembered me; we had met several times over the years. The next day, the consul called to say my visa had arrived.

Before leaving, I went to say goodbye to my host's father, Khalil Tamzali, an elderly gentleman who had owned an olive oil factory in Algeria that had been nationalized. He wished me luck: "You are a brave woman, going back into that hornet's nest!" I left Tunis with a sigh.

Any optimism I felt was short-lived. When I arrived at the airport in Algiers, my passport was retained by the police. I was told to pick it up at the Office for Foreigners at the Central Commissariat in the city. I made several trips to that office, two of which turned into interrogations, but my passport was not returned. Then I received a summons to appear at the Sécurité Militaire headquarters in the Ministry of Defense. It had been two years since I had been hauled off to those same offices and asked to spy on Zohra Sellami, and here we were starting all over again: the same question and the same refusal, recorded.

As soon as I left the SM offices, I called Cherif Belkacem—better known by his *nom de guerre*, Djamel—one part of the three-man brain trust closest to Boumediene, and one of the instigators of the 1965 coup. He was a leading member of government, had headed two key ministries, education and finance, and was a member of the Council of the Revolution, created following the coup. In the 1960s I had been a frequent guest at his famous parties. I knew his gorgeous Swedish wife and his close collaborators. I had also witnessed his descent into heavy drinking and womanizing.

I had Djamel's private number. When I said I needed his help, he invited me to his home the same evening. His reaction was trenchant: no way should I be intimidated and used by the SM. He would take care of my problem, not to worry. The following week, Djamel called to say the matter had been dropped. I then asked him to intervene for the return of my passport and the issuance of a new residence permit.

I had, in the interim, also contacted Simon Malley, the director of the Parisian magazine *Afrique Asie*. I knew him from New York and we had maintained contact over the years. I was a member of the magazine's editorial board and had written articles for it, notably one on the Split that had made a splash in the French-speaking world. Simon spoke to the secretary-general of the president's office; he too was assured that my case would be dropped.

On January 29, I received a summons to appear at the Central Commissariat "to pick up your passport." Mokhtar and I were not suspicious; on the contrary, we figured it meant my dossier had been filed away for good. He needed my car that day and drove me to police headquarters. It was the last time we would see each other for many months. I was deported that afternoon—shipped out on a plane to Paris, a place I was forbidden to enter by edict.

"If they've done that to me, it's not a good sign," Djamel said on the phone that night, "but I'll see what I can do." I took him to mean that he saw himself as a loser in the power game. That the SM had gone over his head had considerable significance for his political future. His star was waning.

I spoke to him occasionally, but he had nothing to report. Then, in July, he called me: "The way is clear. Get yourself a visa. You can come back." I couldn't get to the Algerian consulate fast enough.

On July 23, 1974, I arrived in Algiers in the early afternoon and slid through passport control without a hitch. From the baggage hall, through the glass windows, I saw Mokhtar with Simone and Mohamed Rezzoug. We smiled big smiles of victory and waved. My bag arrived, and as I reached for it I felt a tap on my shoulder. An official in uniform told me to follow him. He asked for my passport and drew a line through the entry stamp. My name was on a list.

I was put on the same plane back to Paris. Air France demanded a return ticket that I refused to buy and the airport authorities did not furnish. The company complained: "The passenger was turned back despite a valid visa." But they took me on board and landed me once again in a country that had me on record as unwanted.

Mokhtar and I spoke that night. "They are ungrateful mother-fuckers," he fumed.

From January to July 1974 I had holed up in the Chapos' apartment on boulevard de l'Hôpital, convinced I would find my way back to Algeria. When I ran out of money I found odd jobs that paid cash, one of which was designing and stringing necklaces for Francine Serfati, my old friend from Algiers. Being interdicted in Paris was not yet a great worry. I remained optimistic.

Eldridge, too, was illegal. Although more cautious in his movements, he was engaging with a swish Parisian crowd that he hoped would edge him closer to political-refugee status. One day in late February he showed up at the Chapos', fit to explode with excitement. He sprawled out on the sofa and poured forth a bewitching tale. He had a new friend, the Gamma photojournalist Marie-Laure de Decker. I had never seen him so beside himself. He was alive with gestures and mimicry and laughter as he described the fantastic lady in bed with him. She was holding a telephone to his ear, then pulling it away to grunt an *hein*, a *oui* or a *non* to the person at the other end of the line: Finance Minister Valéry Giscard d'Estaing. And now Marie-Laure was arranging for the two men to meet.

According to Eldridge, Marie-Laure was as audacious as he was manipulative. On assignment from Gamma to take photos at a meeting of the French cabinet, she rented a soft, swanky mink coat and, making a less-than-discreet entrance into the council room, circled around and snapped photos with angled shots and suggestive thrusts that did not go unnoticed. Before floating out, she dropped her business card in Giscard's palm.

The meeting between Eldridge and Giscard took place. A few weeks later, Eldridge came around to regale me with a description of Giscard's ministerial headquarters and state residence inside the Louvre, along the rue de Rivoli. He described the famous antique desk, crammed full of banknotes. Giscard had questioned him at length about the United States, political practice, personalities, showing special interest in John F. Kennedy. A picture of Kennedy and Giscard hung on the wall behind his desk. He admitted to being a fan. Most important, he promised to arrange for Eldridge and family to be accepted officially in his country.

The president of France, Georges Pompidou, was suffering from a deadly form of cancer; he would die in office. One of his last acts was to replace Raymond Marcellin, the heavy-handed minister of the interior who was something of a liability. Prime Minister Pierre Messmer appointed the more amenable Jacques Chirac to replace him. Giscard jumped at the opportunity: Chirac was minister of the interior for barely two months, but that was enough time to transform Eldridge into a bona fide political refugee in France, with residence permits for himself, his wife and his two children.

I listened in awe to Eldridge's account of the trip to the Préfecture de Police in Giscard's chauffeur-driven ministerial car, and the accommodating routine he went through to receive his official residence card.

Pompidou died in April; Giscard campaigned for the next seven weeks against Mitterrand, leader of the Socialist Party. Eldridge and Marie-Laure kept up their peculiar style of telephone conversation with the new president following his election on May 18. He called her constantly describing the official events. She took a photo of Giscard that became famous: lounging in a low, velvet armchair, legs crossed, watching himself on television the day of his victory.

According to the daily *Le Parisien*, in an article that appeared forty years later on July 22, 2014, Gamma forwarded a series of photos from Marie-Laure de Decker to the national magazine *L'Express* a few days prior to Giscard's inauguration. They were all of the former president—branded as "Valéry Strangelove," a "heartless sentimentalist" in the article—and all taken by her except one, snapped undoubtedly by the future president. According to *Le Parisien*, de Decker "is seated, in a provocative attitude, behind the well-known desk signed by Riesener," the famous eighteenth-century cabinet-maker. When Françoise Giroud, the director of *L'Express*, was shown this photo, she didn't hesitate: "Not for publication . . . Not right away."

I saw less of Eldridge after that. After my forced return to Paris, I called him. We met on the terrace of a café near Châtelet. Kathleen had found a house that was to his liking, and they had settled in. He was flying high, had gotten "his shit together"— one of his favorite expressions. I asked him for help in getting my interdiction in France lifted. He sympathized with my situation and promised to speak to the powers that be. He never got back to me.

Who Was Eldridge Cleaver?

With a note of pride, Eldridge often reminded me that he'd "never been plugged into the system." He meant that he'd never held down a job and collected a regular paycheck, but I figured that his boast went deeper. He was more at home on the streets than with his family. He was a wayward son, a dropout with a catch-all education. He had lived by his wits in and out of prison, a total of fourteen years inside. He learned how to defend himself—however, wherever—using his physical strength and his keen intelligence. He developed the capacity to manipulate others in order to become the kingpin and remain so.

Panthers who have written about their relationship with Eldridge claim that he erected a wall between himself and them. BPP chief David Hilliard, for example, wrote, "I feel shut out by him . . . I can't ever seem to find the man; instead he's obscure, wrapping himself up in mystery."[9] I recognize that side of Eldridge: he cultivated intimidation. He meant to be inaccessible. When I conjure up an image, I see a tall, muscular man looking down at me without bending his head. He raises his brows. His eyelids follow, rise and flatten, partially unveiling smooth green eyes. His arms are crossed. He is able to hold that position indefinitely, unless—or until—he decides to speak. Sometimes a grin develops, he's aware of his effect.

Eldridge made no sacrifices. His own desires were uppermost and had to be assuaged. What others thought of his behavior was of little significance. He was beyond criticism. Where women were concerned, whether it be Beverly Axelrod, his lawyer, to whom he dedicated *Soul on Ice* with "the ultimate of love," Kathleen, the young, passionate SNCC militant he married, or the other powerful women he seduced along the way, he could be ruthless. I was one of many witnesses to the extremes of humiliation and despair that Kathleen suffered, physically and emotionally. When I asked her why she hadn't left him sooner (1981, according to her), she had no convincing reply.

His bestseller *Soul on Ice* provides a close-up of Eldridge and his obsession with sex. He became adept at programming rape. I believe that the book's success served to convince him of his power to transcend the immorality of violating women, or any other reprehensible conduct. He refined the habit of throwing his worst deeds and misdemeanors out on the street for others to pick up and deal with. Rendering his trash public became a survival technique.

Huey Newton, Bobby Seale, and Don Cox may have gained learning from the streets, but they were not "street kids," whatever the general opinion. They had been through high school and enrolled in college. Eldridge came to the BPP straight from the byways of prison. His was a category apart that gave him power.

In 1973, at a time when he was illegal in Paris, Eldridge wrote me to say: "Don't worry. I'll be okay as long as I can get it up." He clearly felt comfortable in France. He knew how to operate, to resist introspection and avoid castigation.

I hesitate to say that he was fond of me. Rather, perhaps, he didn't want to see me hurt. He counted on me for so much. I pressed a lifetime of friends and contacts into service for him. I was his interpreter, both linguistically and for an understanding of the society that harbored him. I gave him news of the outside world. When he had a vocabulary loss, he turned to me for the word or for the meaning. I was less given to compliments than his fans, although I sensed he wanted my approval, especially when we came out of meetings with functionaries, foreign militants, or diplomats. He was far more sensitive than is often imagined, and he was quick to realize that any thought of sex between us had to be suppressed if we were to remain allies.

Eldridge had no qualms about sex: every woman he desired was a legitimate quarry. He didn't hesitate with the women of his best friends and closest allies, essential collaborators, whatever the consequences. The list of damage done is long and, within my own field of knowledge, includes bitterness and vengeance, sorrow and heartache, attempted suicide, and the murder of Kathleen's lover, Rahim. "What is mine is no one else's" was how he justified the murder to the Panthers in Algiers. "He was a goner once he fucked Kathleen."[10]

Over the years Eldridge managed the International Section of the BPP, I watched him grow increasingly stealthy. It was like an illness, an extreme form of self-protection resulting from his background in a violent family and his years of incarceration. In his book *Soul on Fire*, the strange sequel to *Soul on Ice* published in 1978, Eldridge travels through sections of his life, scattering a wagonload of lies and distorted truths. I imagine he was clearing the path to his role as megastar on the religion circuit. The passages about his boyhood, however, are striking and ring true. The family of six children—three girls and three boys, of which Eldridge was the eldest boy—was dragged from Arkansas to Arizona to California by a violent father who terrorized them all, up to the day Eldridge was big enough and powerful enough to destroy him. The father understood it was time to move on, and abandoned home and family.

It's worth remembering that in *Soul on Ice*, Eldridge tangles with James Baldwin over Baldwin's criticism of Norman Mailer's *The White Negro*. Did he identify with Mailer's psychopath? Had his rapes and violence found justification there? Mailer was vicious when aroused, which earned Cleaver's respect, whereas he railed against Baldwin for "the hatred for blacks permeating his writing" and "the most shameful, fanatical, fawning, sycophantic love of the whites that one can find in the writings of any black American writer of note in our time." "Homosexuality is a sickness," Cleaver added.[11] Baldwin understood Mailer and feared the "show" character in his writing. Baldwin eschewed half-truths: "you hear only your own voice," he would admit, "and you begin to drown in this endless duplication of what looks like yourself." It seems Baldwin was deeply affected by Eldridge's attack.

In the end, despite the things about him that I despised—his killer instinct, his womanizing—I admired the man. He was intelligent and articulate. He had a way of keying in on people and events that indicated deep understanding. He put himself inside Richard Nixon's head when he hung a wall at the Embassy with a large diagram of the presidential brain with its preoccupations, which included Vietnam and the antiwar movement, the

Weathermen and, of course, the Black Panther Party. He used language that was devastating: partly political, partly "down" talk, with a little biblical sloganeering mixed in.

I enjoyed being around him. He had a sense of humor; he was reflective. I was flattered to be his confidante. I lived with Eldridge and Malika at the Pointe Pescade apartment for some weeks, when a former boyfriend was stalking me and I feared being alone at home. I observed their tenderness and love. When he left Algiers I suffered loss. I missed him. And yet later, in Paris, once he became legal and was hosting the president of the French Republic's nighttime escapades, he dropped me. When I asked for help to squelch the interdiction and obtain working and residence papers, he promised it but did nothing. It would have been so easy.

I gradually lost interest in Eldridge. When I read that he was designing pants for men to mold around their sex organs, I distrusted his motivation and ridiculed him. When he gave himself up to US justice and returned to the States, I wondered if he'd made a deal. As the *Nation* put it: "Whatever his motives, as an apostate revolutionary he will be a valuable property for the Establishment."[12]

Although his years in the BPP kindled Eldridge's sense of justice, he was also edged with the need to destroy. He could be understanding, but he was not a spokesman for tolerance. While theoretically a team player, he was a loner who made his own laws. When the BPP partnership with Newton and Seale failed, contributing to the destruction of the party, he dug up his past— every man for himself.

Today, I try to see things as they were—without emotion, if that's possible—and accept the obvious: we'd had a relationship that affected me deeply, and that came to an abrupt end through his undoing: he never got back to me, never put his power to use for me in France. In *Newsweek*, on March 17, 1975, Jane Friedman wrote, after interviewing him in Paris: "Somehow now he is less grand than I would have thought."[13]

Kathleen has described the shock of seeing Eldridge in a California courtroom, ten years after their divorce, when she was a member of the legal team defending Elmer "Geronimo" Pratt: "Seeing how he had deteriorated distressed me." In 1994, she stated in an interview with the *San Francisco Chronicle* that "he came back a very unhealthy person, unhealthy mentally, and I don't think he's ever quite recovered."

A few years ago, surfing the Internet, I stumbled upon a filmed interview of Eldridge conducted by Henry Louis Gates Jr. in 1997, one year before Eldridge died. His interpretation of events contained both truths and distortions, as was his game. I wasn't surprised to hear him admit that he, not the cops, had started the shootout that sent him back to prison in 1968. He looked weak and unstrung. He appeared to have pulled himself together for the interview with difficulty.

Yes, as the lady said, less grand.

8

After Algiers

My first thoughts, when I realized that I might never be permitted to enter Algeria again, were of Mokhtar. Was this the end for us? I felt alone in a bubble, afloat, at home neither in France nor in Algeria. When I look back from where I am today, I believe that the shocks I received as a Jewish child in an anti-Semitic Christian society had somehow prepared me for the blows that lambasted me later in life. Desperate and unhappy, but held together with a strong sense of survival. And *voilà*, Mokhtar came to Paris that summer. We spent the glorious month of August in the city and in the south of France. We made plans. He would join me as soon as he could get his affairs in order. I felt so lucky. I was giddy.

The day I was thrust onto the plane in Algiers, I left an entire life behind: friends, work, car, apartment, clothes, jewelry, furniture, correspondence, archives, a collection of paintings and prints, photos . . . and, more important, Mokhtar. I was estranged from my own existence. Mokhtar and I maintained our connection by mail, but our natures made us both inordinately shy with words that express sentiments. Mo, my ever-vigilant upstairs neighbor, told me that some weeks after my departure, the police arrived, sirens blasting, to empty my apartment. The chief of police, Ahmed Draia, had allocated the place to a woman in his entourage and often came to visit. Had I been packaged and dispatched so that the top cop could occupy an apartment? There are people who would suggest as much.

I remember every detail of that apartment: where each painting hung, the Hiroshige print, the Vietnamese woodcut that Trần Hoài Nam gave me, Mohamed Bouzid's pastoral oil painting. In my mind's eye, I can still put my hand on the Chinese letter opener that Eldridge brought back from Beijing, the Danish wine glasses that Zohra gave me on my birthday, the mink hat from Ahmed Laidi when Ben Bella's delegation returned from Moscow, the Japanese paper lantern over the round oak dining-room table that Nicole Chapo shipped from France, the Italian brocaded chairs with metal stitching that I bought on the sidewalk in the lower Casbah.

Mokhtar arrived in early November. He had resigned from his consultancy job in a state company, sold my Austin Mini, and turned his apartment over to his nephew Nasserdine and family. He warned his friends that Algeria was racing at top speed toward total control by forces of darkness. *Soutien critique*, or constructive criticism, the watchword of the moment for progressives, was a compromise that would only provide fuel for the engines of reaction. For democratic thought and process to take hold required a progressive insurrectionary movement. That was not going to happen. He embraced his relatives and friends and said goodbye.

Paris too had a housing shortage, and we could show no proof of income. Who would rent to us? Mokhtar still had a student visa from his days at the Sorbonne, but I was nonexistent in France. In January friends lent us an apartment on the rue du Faubourg Saint-Antoine, a fifth-floor walkup without heat or hot water. We took advantage of every dinner invitation to clean up and shower and, at night, cuddled under a heap of blankets. If we didn't find a way of quashing my interdiction, we would have to leave France. There would be no way to work legally, to travel without fear, to open a bank account, to garner any of the benefits of residency.

On the afternoon of February 1, 1975, Mokhtar came back to the apartment with a rolled copy of *Le Monde* that he kept pounding in the palm of his hand, on his face a smile of secret knowledge and contentment. The front page announced that Yvon Bourges had been named Giscard's minister of defense. Hadn't I known one Hervé Bourges when he was special counselor to Ben Bella, prior to the coup d'état? Indeed I had, but where to find him now? And was he related to Yvon Bourges? I had heard he was heading an institute for the press in Paris.

I skipped down the five flights of stairs and ran to the pay telephone on the place de la Bastille. I called information and they came up with a number. When I reached the press center, I was told that Hervé Bourges was in Cameroon founding a school of journalism, and wouldn't be back for months. They gave me his wife's number. When I said I had known her husband in Algeria, she told me to call back in April, when he would be home for Easter.

We were getting lucky. Mokhtar's nephew Brahim had a friend with an apartment to rent who was willing to take a chance on us. In March, we moved to a small one-bedroom on the rue Flatters in the fifth arrondissement. Mokhtar contacted an old friend, Annie Cohen, who he remembered was well connected in the Socialist Party. Annie brought round someone from the staff of a southern préfecture who was in a position to make inquiries about me. In no time, she returned with information: "This case is too hot to handle, stay away from it," her friend had been warned.

We were not ready to quit. On the contrary, we were galvanized. We connected with another friend, Nicole Landau, who knew people at the Ministry of the Interior. The commissaire read my file and got back to her: I was down as an "international terrorist." We would have to go to the top if we hoped to lift the interdiction, he told her. So now we knew.

I rendezvoused with Hervé Bourges shortly after he arrived from Cameroon. Yes, Yvon Bourges was his cousin, but he had a better contact for what I required: Bernard Stasi, former minister of overseas territories, was a friend from grammar school days who was particularly sensitive to problems of immigration and human rights. He was the mayor of Épernay, the capital of Champagne, but also had an office in Paris. "I will write to him," Bourges said, and he did.[1]

Shortly thereafter, Bernard Stasi received me at his Parisian office, 40 cours Albert-1er. A small man with a limp, he smiled and greeted me warmly, in no way officious. He asked to hear my story. I told it; there were no interruptions. When I stopped talking, he looked at me squarely and said, "I will help you." I told him I had heard my case required going to the top. He replied, "That's where I intend to go. I will be in touch with you."

And he was, sending me the originals and copies of all correspondence concerning my file. The first letter from Michel Poniatowski, the minister of the interior, was dated May 15, 1975: "I will have my services examine this case." The interdiction was quickly abrogated, but it took over a year for me to become a legal resident of France—on September 29, 1976. Why so long? Stasi reported that the interdiction was the result of a request from the FBI.

そのそ

Mokhtar and I borrowed key money for a minute jewelry shop on the Left Bank, three steps down from street level, with low rent and a low ceiling that kept Mokhtar bent in two to navigate in and out. The shop's name was Patchanga, a French way of spelling the 1960s Cuban music and dance genre of pachanga.

I had learned some basic techniques of jewelry-making from Francine Serfati and now took an evening class with Anne Boline, a highly qualified metalworker who taught me to solder and set stones. It was enough to qualify as an artisan. I produced ethnic-style necklaces, bracelets, earrings, and rings using decorative stones and handmade silver pieces and beads. Mokhtar did the bookkeeping and learned to string necklaces. We made a living and even bought an attic apartment in the building next door. We ran the shop for some eight years before opening a second boutique on the Right Bank, just off place Vendôme. In 1983 we sold the first shop and, at the end of 1989, the second.

One day on vacation on the Côte d'Azur, we were struck with the thought that we did not want to spend the rest of our lives stringing necklaces. Mokhtar was preoccupied with the need for Algerians of his and future generations to know their own history. It was not taught in French schools, and it would be many years before independent Algeria produced reliable textbooks. There and then he decided to write a history of Algeria for young people and those with minimal schooling, like many of his friends and comrades from the liberation army.

Not to be outdone, I told him that the day we stopped stringing beads and soldering earrings, I would restart life as a painter. My high-school art teacher had tried to convince me that art was my destiny. I had ignored her advice at the time, but now I was ready. I started evening classes with two beautiful artists, Isabelle Forestier and Anne Rouillon.

Mokhtar's talent as a researcher and writer was recognized by two of the top French publishers. His first book, an illustrated history for teenagers, *Aux premiers siècles de l'Islam* (The Rise of Islam) was published by Hachette in 1985 and translated into English, Indonesian, German, Japanese, Polish, and Portuguese. A second illustrated book, *L'Égypte au présent*, came out in 1989. Éditions Nathan published *Les Arabes au temps de l'âge d'or* (The Arabs in the Golden Age) in 1991 and *Maroc, Algérie, Tunisie: les pays du Maghreb* in 1992, also illustrated history books for young readers. A revised edition of his first book with a new title, *Les débuts de l'Islam*, came out in 2003.

Still refusing to be outdone, I published, in 1990, an illustrated book for young readers on the American Civil War, *La Guerre de Sécession*, with Éditions Nathan. In 1992, for Albin Michel, another French publisher, I wrote and produced an illustrated book with Yann Le Béchec, a very fine artist, called *New York Quartiers Noirs*. I published two travel guides with Hippocrene Books of New York in 1991 and 1993, *Insiders' Guide to Paris* and *Language & Travel Guide to France*. Finally, *Paris: An Illustrated History* was published by Hippocrene in 2002. After a trip to Buenos Aires in 2005, I illustrated a series of my own Japanese-style tanka poems for a chapbook.

As soon as we sold the second Parisian shop in 1989, I became active with the Palestinian liberation movement. Ellen Wright and I demonstrated every Saturday at place du Châtelet, where we were regularly insulted by passersby and motorists, one of whom tried to run her car into the militants on the square. Mokhtar and I formed a strong bond with Régine Fiorani, an exemplary activist, and her Palestinian partner. When the group broke up in 1990, following Régine's departure for Marseille, I demonstrated at Les Halles with Americans Against the War, the war at the time being the Gulf War.

My father, who had never been sick for a day, gradually lost his memory and died in 1989 at the age of ninety-one. He still recognized me, although he couldn't come up with my name. He asked my mother Mildred how many children they had. We brought her to Paris in the hope that she would live with us, but she found Paris too strange and herself too old to adapt. She returned to Florida until our cousins Sondra and Steve Koff found her a comfortable residency in Syracuse, New York, that was a few minutes from their home.

In 1991, just before she left Florida, Mokhtar and I married in Fort Lauderdale. My mother attended the ceremony at a city marriage bureau along some railroad tracks. We celebrated with a boat ride around the bay. We had dinner at an elegant Italian restaurant and, back at the apartment, she sang songs from the 1920s until late into the night.

Mokhtar and I decided it was time to leave France, where racism was a daily presence. In the streets and the metro, racial profiling of North Africans and Black Africans by special, heavily armed police units was unremitting. He applied for an immigrant visa to the United States that was granted in 1994, and we left for Syracuse.

We went immediately to Mildred's bedside. I had moved her from the residency to a nursing home when she became too weak to fend for herself. The nurses at the home had informed our cousins that Mildred imagined she was pregnant, and had announced that her baby was due. She was one of the bright lights at the home: the nurses loved her and played along with her fantasy. The day after she announced the baby's birth, they brought a large doll and placed it next to her bed.

She was delighted to see us. When I bent down to kiss her I felt the burst of a tear on her cheek. When Mokhtar followed me into the room, she raised her arms to him and grabbed on as hard as she could. She scolded me for not arriving sooner—it was time to give the baby a name! We lobbed names back and forth until she settled on Harold. "Harold Mississippi!" she exclaimed.

The following day, as we were putting on our coats to return to the nursing home for a visit, we received a call at our cousins' house: Mildred had died as she was readying for lunch. We were shocked, sad and disturbed. We like to think she had been waiting for us. Mokhtar and I buried her ashes in the woods behind the Koffs' home. Mokhtar said prayers from the Quran in Arabic, and we laid her to rest. We planted a magnolia a few feet away; it is now a large, beautiful tree that we have visited many times. At the thought of her, our eyes would fill with tears and we would hold on to each other.

We moved to New York. Mokhtar enrolled in an ESL course at Columbia Teachers College. I signed up for classes at the Art Students League and painted all week long. I now have a website (elainemokhtefi.com) and a number of exhibitions under my belt, the most recent in 2017 in Paris, at La Petite Galerie on rue de Seine. I also have a studio in Harlem that I share with my dear friends Montserrat Daubón and Pedro Villalta.

As long as our legs held out, Mokhtar and I attended antiwar and Free Palestine demonstrations in New York and Washington. Sadly, the leaders of our country were not willing to listen to us. We took part in climate marches, Occupy Wall Street and antiracist mobilizations, never forgetting the Palestinians, our heart-of-hearts issue.

Mokhtar returned to Algeria once a year to see his family and visit the graves of his mother and father in Berrouaghia, his hometown. "*Ils m'ont donné la vie,*" he would say. (They gave me life.)

Mokhtar died on April 4, 2015. He was eighty years old. Ten days earlier, barely able to raise his body from the bed, he dressed, leaned on a cane, and slowly climbed the slight incline to Broadway. We hailed a taxi and crossed the entire city from west to east to reach the Algerian consulate near the UN. He wanted to finish his business with Algeria, to provide his nephew Djamel with an authorization to act in his name for family affairs.

The consulate consisted of a drab, ordinary room, despite the bright red, white, and green Algerian flag and an outsize photo of Bouteflika; chairs lined the walls. There was no receptionist, just a sign indicating a bell to ring. Gradually, other Algerians arrived: a "hip" student, a couple from Philadelphia with a newborn baby, a businessman, a Berber family accompanied by an elderly lady wearing a traditional scarf wrapped around her head like a turban. Conversation was slow to take off, then quickly became personal and animated. Within minutes we knew where everyone was from, details of their lives, even a few political opinions. Agents came in. They met our demands politely and kindly. While previous conversations had been in mixed French and Arabic, they spoke Arabic with some English. Here, I thought, was a "little Algeria" on the East River.

We took another taxi back across the city. Mokhtar was smiling, pleased with that last taste of Algeria. There was something basic that he recognized on both sides of the barrier—among the petitioners and among the agents. They had all been weaned on the same sense of dignity and equality. Everyone had felt it and identified. That evening he explained to our friend Amara Lakhous, the Algerian writer, that there are bonds that can never be cast off: "Algeria lies under our feet and in our hearts until death."

A few days later, Mokhtar rummaged through an old box, where I store mementos of our militant past, for a button inscribed with the words: "I am a world citizen." Every day thereafter he pinned that badge on his shirt. Mokhtar's gestures and statements were not offhand; with his badge, he was not contradicting himself. He was making a final statement, charting the future for us all.

The youngest of six boys, Mokhtar was born and raised in Berrouaghia (the Asphodels), a village in the plateau region south of Algiers. He was the only one of the brothers to graduate from high school, a French *lycée*. It was there that he began organizing for Algerian independence, creating and recruiting for an FLN clandestine cell. In 1957 he joined the liberation army, receiving training as a radio operator in the newly formed signal corps. He was deployed in the southern war zone at the head of a transmissions detachment.

In 1962, Mokhtar was elected president of UGEMA, the national student association, and tasked with its reorganization in the newly liberated country. He attended college in Algiers and obtained masters' degrees in sociology, economics and law in Paris. He held positions in the Ministry of Agriculture and Agrarian Reform—in charge of training and education—as well as in several state companies. Later, in Paris, he wrote illustrated books for young readers on Islam, the Arab world, and North Africa.

Mokhtar had given his life to Algeria. He and his comrades joined the liberation army prepared to die for their flag and more—for an idea, for justice. Following independence, to see the ideals they had fought for soiled, spit upon, was more than he could bear. When I was deported for refusing to become an informer for the military police, it was the final blow. As he wrote at the time: "My last illusions are gone. Exile remains the ultimate solution when mediocrity and feudalism triumph and return as our judges."

Mokhtar lived for twenty years in Paris and twenty years in New York. Paris often tore at his entrails. He felt surrounded by the racism of his youth. He was happy in New York, despite the frightening lack of sympathy for Palestine. He felt free here, and found peace in writing. His final book, *J'étais français-musulman. Itinéraire d'un soldat de l'ALN*, was a memoir of his life, telling how he became a nationalist, a militant, and a soldier of the Algerian liberation struggle.[2] When he learned that Éditions Barzakh of Algiers would publish the manuscript in 2016, he felt the warm rush of accomplishment.

A few days after his eightieth birthday, Mokhtar learned that he had liver cancer. "I want to go home with Elaine and die there," he told his doctor. "My life is behind me." His last piece of writing was a short text in English: "I had a wonderful life," it declared. "I don't want to waste Elaine's time and mine going to hospitals and clinics. We adore each other and want to protect our happiness."

Mokhtar's last words to me: "*Je t'embrasse.*"

In 1990, after ten years in exile, Zohra and Ahmed Ben Bella returned to Algeria to live out their lives. I never heard from them. Zohra died of cancer in 2010; Ben Bella died at the age of ninety-five in 2012. Both were honored with state funerals.

All these forty-four years my name has remained on a list, barring me from entry into the country. A few days before this book went to press, the Consulate General of Algeria in New York informed me that authorization had been received to issue a visa in my name. I am profoundly happy and may once again walk the streets, breathe the air and the light of Algeria, and embrace my family and friends.

My story with Algeria has invaded and occupied my being forever. I was one of the dreamers who came to build a more perfect world. I believed in the Algerian peoples' heart and soul, throughout the war and in the reconstruction of the battered country. In return, I received affection, a sense of acknowledgement, a home. I have never met an Algerian who has not been scarred from so much injustice, so much misery, all still unresolved. My first act in the morning, in my apartment on the Upper West Side of New York, after I have nodded good morning to the portrait of Mokhtar on the wall, is to open the computer to *El Watan*, the Algiers daily in French. I am moved by the exceedingly proper language and smile at the expressions from another era, the manner of presentation so old-fashioned for a reader of the *New York Times*. In every gathering, I seek them out, Algerians young and old: they are people with a sense of the past, and I go back with them, and remember. I am young again.

Afterword

An American Childhood

I was a Depression baby, born in December 1928, a few months before the Crash.

My first memory of myself is a child standing on a chair, with her head pushing against the window of a second-floor apartment. She is looking down to the street below and bawling, her mouth contorted, her face oily with tears. My mother said I couldn't possibly remember this: I was only two years old when we lived over the dry-goods store that she and my father managed in Hempstead, Long Island. She did admit that she might have left me alone in the apartment when it rained or snowed. She used to laugh about the customer who came into the shop one day and damned the hard-hearted woman who left her child unattended in a baby carriage on the sidewalk in zero-degree weather. For me the snapshot of the child in the window is as clear as the day was cloudy, an image in black, white, and gray.

When the store in Hempstead closed, everything we had was gone: apartment, business, money. Relatives in Brooklyn took us in, Uncle John and Aunt Clara. My father had an entrepreneurial spirit and convinced Uncle John to loan him some cash. With two partners—buddies from the old Jewish quarter of

Bedford-Stuyvesant, Brooklyn—he rented space and began jobbing textiles. When the business took off, we moved into a private house with a rock garden on Narrows Avenue. I was five, close enough to six to be admitted to first grade. After school, I played with the neighborhood kids on the dark, greasy, abandoned docks along the Narrows, the waterway leading into New York's harbor. When I arrived home, soiled, wet, and cringing, my mother would scream at me: "Stay away from those docks! You don't know how to swim! You'll kill me yet!"

On Sunday afternoons, we joined the neighbors sitting on the grass above the docks. We waved to the people lining the decks of the ocean liners as they made their majestic passage through the Narrows to their moorings on the Hudson. We had reentered the mainstream. That is, until the day my dad arrived at the warehouse to find the stock and the partners gone and the joint bank account cleaned out. It was the only time I saw my father cry. He was not sentimental: he, the hard-working man rising from the pits, forced once more to admit defeat and to scrounge. He declared bankruptcy.

It was then that he made the decision to get out of dry goods and out of New York City: away from his family, from his former friends and business pals who had screwed him, and from the Jews. According to him, the Jews were to blame for his losses and our state of emergency, not the government, nor the banks, nor the economy, nor a few lowlifes. We would be dependent on no one; we would go it alone.

We started making excursions to small towns in upstate New York. We'd walk along the main streets, check any empty stores, and seek out the owners. In Brewster, we hit on a small, empty shop: "See next door," said the sign in the window. My father contacted the owner and came away with a done deal. Happy, we sauntered along the street to get the feel of the town and walked smack into the large window of Aaron Fineberg Dry Goods. Fineberg—that sounded Jewish, so we went in. (My father was never short on contradictions.)

"Charlie Klein. This is my wife Mildred and my daughter."

If there was one thing Charlie Klein knew something about, it was dry goods: it was in a dry-goods store in Brooklyn that my parents had met, he the traveling salesman, she the clerk. In Hempstead, dry goods had been their retail business. His venture into jobbing was also in dry goods. This was Charlie's chance to talk about his business past with a colleague and to ask questions about life in Brewster. In the shop down the street, he would specialize in women's clothing, not cloth.

They talked all afternoon. At closing time, Mr. Fineberg invited us to come home with him and meet his wife Rose. We ended up living with Aaron and Rose in their house on Prospect Street for close to three years.

It was the beginning of summer and my parents needed time to settle in, fit out the shop, and buy merchandise, so they deposited six-year-old me at my maternal grandparents' small dairy farm in upstate Connecticut, a place called Chestnut Hill, a road without a town, not even a mark on the map. They explained that it would be easier for them if they navigated alone. I rustled within, so sure I was that they were happier without me.

I stayed on the farm that summer, the entire next school year, and part of the following summer. My parents arrived for the day from time to time and we exchanged letters. Mine were appalling: "How are you, I am fine" letters in chaotic handwriting. I attended the one-room schoolhouse a mile down the road, passing from second grade to fourth without a blink. I walked to school with the Berkowitz kids from the farm across the way. We passed the Kaplans, who were chicken farmers, then the brick synagogue, and next was the school. It was a straight road, no curves.

The small community in Chestnut Hill was made up of poor Polish Jews attempting to survive on poor, stone-pecked land. Old Mr. Fuller owned the farm down the slope below us. His land extended to the railroad tracks, where a freight train passed occasionally. At the crossing was Mr. Loomis's general store. It was the only store for miles, dark and dirty. I would go there to buy gum and duck out in a hurry.

When school let out, the days were endless. There were few cars, no people on the road, and no one to play with—except the Berkowitz kids who were numerous and sufficed for themselves. My pastime was waiting for the postman. In the farmhouse it was as silent as a church prayer room. How much time could I spend watching Grandma roll out noodles or knead bread? In the afternoons, Grandpa would lie down in the ground-floor bedroom and Grandma, who was his second wife, would read softly to him in Yiddish from the Jewish *Daily Forward*. Then they would take a nap.

Grandpa was blind. My job was to walk him down the driveway to the barn. He would feel and fumble his way along the two rows of cow stalls and fill the metal container attached to each stall with grain from a long wooden bin. I can still recall the dry, dull odor that filled our nostrils when we lifted the lid of the bin. Grandpa was a tall man with some girth around the middle, white hair, a white mustache, and a long white beard. He held his pants up with broad suspenders. We had a mangy dog, something like a police dog, that I fed with leftovers from the kitchen.

My room was on the second floor of the farmhouse, a low-ceilinged room with two double beds with metal frames and a chest of drawers. At night I could hear the wind blowing, the branches of the large maples out front slamming against the porch. I slept in the farthest bed and turned into the wall. I whiled away hours in the unheated ground-floor living room playing tunes on the piano. "Oh, Genevieve" was my favorite; I would sing along undisturbed and loud, even though I couldn't carry a tune, but no one minded.

Grandma cooked on a huge black wood-burning stove. She made her own noodles and blintzes and wonderful pies with huckleberries I picked in the fields. She felt for the abandoned child and would take me in her arms and kiss and cradle me.

Uncle Arthur, the last of their eight children, was sixteen, in high school in Willimantic, five miles away. Evenings, we would go together into the pastures to bring home the dozen cows. Once he'd milked them he was off to the city on his bike. He played the clarinet and loved to dance.

When the membership of the synagogue was short a man to make the ten required for a *minyan* on Saturdays, someone would arrive running to drag Arthur out of bed. He would take me along and sit me down beside him in one of the front pews, not in the cordoned-off seats in the back where a few women sat. I didn't understand what was going on, but I was happy spending the morning with Arthur. We adored each other: in the barn he would squirt me with spray from a teat. I would try and try my little hands at milking, and he would tease me, but the truth was he was rarely home.

I began to cry. I would sit down in the big kitchen and cry, go out on the porch and cry, into the yard and cry. I was a mess, so Arthur wrote to my parents. When they came, my mother took me upstairs to the bedroom and sat me down on the bed. She asked why I was crying. All I could think of saying was, "I was afraid Grandma was going to die."

When I finally returned to Brewster, home was a second-floor room with a double bed and a cot in the corner for me. Rose and Aaron Fineberg slept downstairs in a room off the large dining-living room.

Rose, in her mid-to-late sixties, had a gaunt face and pale green eyes. She bent as she walked, with a slow gait, and sometimes a cane. Her dresses were hand-knit two-piece affairs that clung somewhat, falling to mid-calf. She taught my mother how to transform Yiddish into German and they spoke German together. With me and my father she spoke English, as did Aaron. Every evening, Aaron wrapped a shawl around his shoulders and prayed, moving his head back and forth in a reverent bobbing motion. There was no synagogue in Brewster, so he adapted. The dry-goods store remained open on Saturdays.

Rose showed Mildred how to make dill pickles and mustard pickles and how to can the green tomatoes from Aaron's garden in Mason jars. The kitchen was big and square, and at the end of the summer open barrels of seasoned vinegar-brine veggies trembled in the corners. Through the kitchen door we could see Aaron's large vegetable garden. He tended it patiently and in silence, as he did most things. Between the garden and the house was a small porch. Many a day, one or two vagabonds would come around to that back porch, hats in hand, and ask for something to eat. Rose and Mildred would put out plates of food. Whatever their guests' attire, they showed no fear and turned no one away. The men, unkempt, carrying at most a bag flung over their shoulders, crouched down to sit on the porch step and eat. When they returned the empty plates, they tipped their caps before walking back down the driveway. They rarely spoke. What was there to say?

Not long after we settled in Brewster, my father decided to become an egg broker. He made contact with farms in the region, bought cases of eggs, and delivered them door to door in Brooklyn on Sundays. We followed an itinerary through the borough, exchanging dozens of "fresh country eggs" for a few dollars' profit: brown or white was the customer's choice. Until one Sunday, when disaster struck in the form of an accident on the highway: we landed in a ditch, half our load of eggs smashed. Despite the damage, we got back on the road and delivered the survivors, but that was the end of Charlie Klein, egg broker.

At eight years old, I entered the fourth grade. Life changed. I made friends with other girls. I walked out of the house in the morning with my metal lunch box and wasn't back until suppertime. On Saturdays, I played with Shirley, the Main Street doctor's daughter; we became tight, best friends. She was tall for a nine-year-old and had a boy's slim, hard build and a pug nose. Next to her, I was a dark, skinny runt. We went to the library together and read the same books. I couldn't get enough of Shirley and her family. Mine was lugubrious by comparison.

Ms. Vanderburgh, Shirley's mother, took Shirley, her two siblings, and me to New York one Saturday. We rode the ferry to the Statue of Liberty and climbed the steps one by one into the crown. In the streets of lower Manhattan, we ate charlotte russe pastry in a little cardboard cup whose bottom moved up with the push of our fingers. The elastic on Ms. Vanderburgh's panties gave way and they slid to the ground in front of the pastry vendor. She bent down, picked them up, and threw them into her handbag; then, looking at the vendor, she laughed. We all burst out laughing.

☙❧

When my Brooklyn grandfather died, my parents left me overnight at Shirley's, and her nanny took me with her and her siblings to church. "Pray for your grandpa," she whispered in my ear. Pray? I didn't know any prayers. And for what? I hardly knew my grandpa. My only memory is of him leaning against the wall alongside the icebox in the large kitchen on the ground floor of the family brownstone in Bedford-Stuyvesant. He never smiled and barely talked. He seemed unaffected by the noise and jabber in that kitchen. My aunts didn't talk, they shrieked. They covered me with kisses and never stopped pinching, but Grandpa never embraced me. He was sour. Years later, I learned he had rectal cancer and suffered unbearable pain.

Living with a family had its drawbacks, and sharing a room with my parents was often rough. The house was old-fashioned, somewhat musty, like the Finebergs themselves. I couldn't invite friends over. I didn't have a room of my own where we could play, and my mother wasn't home most of the day.

The worst was when my parents fought. I had no place to hide. "For Christ's sake, Charlie! Stop that! You're not a bit funny! I'm telling you! Leave me alone!" "What's your problem? Get down off your high horse!" They scared the shit out of me: What if one of them walked out? Where would that leave me?

When I think of my parents, I wonder how well I knew them. My mother never finished primary school: as soon as she learned to read and write, Grandpa pulled her from the classroom to take care of the younger children, three half-sisters and a half-brother. When she was no longer needed on the farm, she left for Brooklyn and found work as a salesperson in the dry-goods store where she met my father. She was tall for the times, five foot six, slim, and attractive, with curly blondish hair, a strong nose, and pale blue eyes, large and watery like a wading pool. She had elegance and good taste, as well as a ripe sense of responsibility. Many years later, in 1971, sitting on the shaded terrace of a restaurant in the quiet hills above Algiers, she told me that her mother had died when she was five, in 1910. It was from an abortion gone bad. Grandpa brought her to the hospital one last time and her mother said: "Mildred, be a good girl." And so she was, all her life.

After one year of high school, my father dropped out and went to work as a delivery boy carrying typewriters to customers for a few hours' or a few days' rental. He was the oldest of five children and felt he had to provide for the others; Grandpa was a carpenter, at times a builder, and always a heavy gambler. Many a night there was nothing in the larder. My father grew up angry. He could draw and sew and had a flair for color and harmony. He liked to dance. I had the feeling he would have loved to let go, holler, have a ball, but life was too serious. He was dark and short, with an athletic build. He loved me dearly. I was "his girl."

My parents were mostly happy with each other; we formed an enclosed, self-sufficient family. They were atheists; today they would be called "non-practicing Jews." My mother was devastated when—in 1989, at the age of ninety-one, no longer walking, his memory dissolved—my father died. She no longer had a role. No one needed her. She and I scattered his ashes on the golf course where he could be found every day at sunup. It was downstairs from their Florida apartment in a gated community to which they retired. They left all the rest, even their memories, behind. It was as though every other experience had been a build-up for this time of life. On leaving New York for small-town USA, they had known they would remain unrooted wherever they settled. They had started on the bottom rung, had worked hard and saved their money, and were living comfortably in the Florida sun. Putting down roots was my job. I did it wherever I lived, throughout my life. I integrated.

At the end of 1938, just when things were picking up for us in Brewster, the shop's landlord asked us to leave. He wanted the shop back. By then we had a secondhand Oldsmobile and we decided to start afresh somewhere else: California! We were ready to venture out, far out. California was the twentieth-century Eldorado that starry-eyed immigrants and desperados from the East Coast, the South, the Midwest, rushed to inhabit. They were the new pioneers, beckoned by fertile land and burgeoning cities along a sparkling coast. But, no, someone sat next to my father on a train to New York and convinced him that California was for the birds—Texas was the future.

So to Texas we went. We loaded the trunk and back seat of the Oldsmobile with clothes and sparse belongings and headed for Dallas, my father at the wheel day and night. I have memories of passing through a mountainous area, the narrow road lined with wood shacks and obvious signs of poverty, people shabbily dressed, ill-kempt and unsmiling, who stared at us, the rare passing car. I sunk deep into my seat. When we hit the South and segregation, we again saw deep poverty; we sped along the roads, stopping only when required. We took breaks a few times in cities at boarding houses. There, we were shaken out of our silence and the boredom of the road: we sat at tables in a room with other people, like in a restaurant, and talked and laughed with the boarders.

In Dallas, we met some Mexican businessmen who sent us to the region along the lower Gulf, close to the Mexican border, that they said would be booming with the arrival of a major army base. We canvassed the area, even walked barefoot across the Rio Grande into Mexico through puddles and sand at low water level, coming back over the bridge to Brownsville, as simple as that. We chose Harlingen—I can't say why. We rented a rather large-sized store and a freshly painted apartment with a room for my parents and a room for me. My room was full of light, but I never closed the door. I didn't feel at home.

I had just turned ten. It was mid-year when I started school. There, it was made clear to me that no one talked to Miguel, no one played with him. Miguel was the only Mexican in our sixth-grade class. Though I wasn't the object of a boycott, no one came home to play in my brightly painted room. I had two stains: I was Jewish and from the North. Skinny, brown Miguel and I bonded. We played catch, marbles, yo-yo, and we jumped rope together until it was time for supper. I still have the drawing he gave me when we left Harlingen: it's buried in a closet with old love letters and report cards. Can a ten-year-old be said to have a first love? If so, Miguel was mine.

Harlingen was not the answer to our quest for a town with a prosperous future, at least not in the 1930s. At the end of the school year we packed up, got into the Oldsmobile, and drove back north. I spent the summer of 1939 again in Chestnut Hill on my grandparents' farm, while Mildred and Charlie went looking for a shop to rent. Gone were the dreams of new frontiers.

I have happy memories of that summer: cousins from New York were there on vacation and some kids who were summer boarders. The farm had started taking in paying guests hungry for a breath of country air. Our upscale Brooklyn relatives sent their poor relations to eat Grandma's wholesome kosher food for a week or two and sit under the leafy maples on the bright green lawn. The kids were my domain. The bedroom with the two double beds became a nightly playground for four of us to tickle and tease. During the day we helped pitch hay, building up the pile on the wagon and balancing ourselves at the top, slipping and tipping from the fields to the barn. Once we'd stacked the hay in the loft, Uncle Arthur would pile us all into the emptied wagon and drive the horses to the lake four miles away. We bumped along dirt roads, then ran for the water.

We ended up in another small town, Ridgefield, Connecticut. In my seventh-grade class there was a "colored" boy to whom no one ever spoke, despite his good looks and the sweetest smile. He was so sure no one would talk to him that he walked into the classroom with his head turned to the wall. What a look of surprise lit his face when I first said hello. It didn't amount to a friendship, but there was now something between us and we always acknowledged each other.

The town referred to me as "the little Jewish girl." I think I was the only Jew in our public school; at any rate, I was the only child in the school who remained silent during the Lord's Prayer. My mother said it was not "our" prayer. What "our" prayer was I never knew, nor, I daresay, did my parents. It was in Ridgefield that I was subjected to the epithet "Christ-killer" for the first time. In Brewster I had belonged to the Girl Scouts, and sold more Girl Scout cookies than any member of the tribe. When I tried to join in Ridgefield, the scout leader refused me. She was clear about it: "no Jews."

Both parents worked long hours in the shop, six days a week. Our one pastime was to visit relatives, two hours away in the Berkshires, or two hours away in Brooklyn on Sundays. Like all kids in those years in small towns across America, our pastimes were outdoor sports. Only pouring rain or blizzards could quarantine us.

I became a soda jerk at the fountain in the cigar store. I had girlfriends and boyfriends and dates for the proms, a major test for a high-school girl. It seems crazy, but I believe my parents never worried about me. Amazing, because we were kids, not little adults. We knew next to nothing about the world outside our town, about sex or psychology. Kissing was our preoccupation, the ultimate act. I remember dancing with a classmate and feeling something hard push against my body. It happened every time I danced with him, but I was too ignorant to know or to ask.

Ours was an era of radio with Jack Armstrong, the All-American Boy, of Saturday movies with Tom Mix, Tarzan, the Lone Ranger . . . uncomplicated heroes. We listened to the radio: weekday evenings our parents turned on the news, and on Sundays we sat around the living room devouring the latest episode in the lives of our role models, *One Man's Family*. Doors were not locked and neighbors could be counted on. As children, we were living on the boundaries of an adult world in which we had confidence. The future was a straight line from school to marriage to parenthood.

My first work experience was as a high-school sports reporter— a volunteer job—for the *Ridgefield Press*. I have to believe that I was already deliberate and partisan to the extreme: someone from out of town once remarked that my articles lauded the local teams to an extent that made a home-team loss read like a win. The best part of the job was riding the bus for the out-of-town games: just me and the boys.

The summer of my junior year, I had my first paying job, arranging in alphabetical order the contact cards of the insurance and real-estate broker whose office was adjacent to my parents' store. He said I had done a good job, then gave my pay—fifteen huge dollars—to my father. I never saw them again. I protested, but all I got was a shrug. Dad thought I was too young to handle money, and money was sacred.

At the bowling alley in Ridgefield, in a basement locale on Main Street, one of the hangouts for teenagers after school and on weekends, I introduced charged subjects like racism. The town practiced a form of segregation. Two Black families lived in the shacks along the railroad tracks. We all knew that no one on our beautiful tree-lined streets would rent to them. Why? It was wartime and we were for democracy and against the Nazis, weren't we? So why were Blacks treated like creatures outside the human race? Weren't they in the army? Didn't the North fight for them to be free?

Perhaps that was my way of protecting "the little Jewish girl," by broadening the dialogue. I had little idea of what being Jewish meant—neither the rituals nor the holidays nor the jokes. My mother knew Yiddish and translated it into English for my father, who had forgotten the language that he was raised in. Some feat, I now say to myself.

My friends at school, at the bowling alley, or later at the bars over the state line in New York, where you could drink at age eighteen, were generous. For them I was strange, even unique. I had come from somewhere else, out of nowhere, perhaps. I was an only child. I got good grades without trying. I didn't go to their church, or to any church. They were from large, immigrant Italian and Irish families where noise and talk were life.

One evening, a group of us went over the New York state line to a roadside inn where there was a jukebox and we could dance. Some friends arrived with a tall, handsome Black man called

Matt, who worked on one of the estates in the hills outside Ridgefield. When a pretty redhead came over and asked him to dance, Matt retreated, his excuse "two left feet." To me, he whispered: "I want to get out of here alive!"

I started thinking of Ridgefield as a "one-horse town". My buddies and I swore that we would be off to the wide world after high school: we were not going to be confined to a village that offered little in the way of employment or modernity. Women were restricted to nursing or teaching or secretarial work. We saw ourselves as the vanguard, unlike our mothers who, except for mine, had never had a job.

Our music was swing, the product of the big bands. We became "bobby-soxers." With two or three girlfriends, I would sneak off to New York City on the nine o'clock bus, arriving in Times Square two hours later, in time for the midday show at the Paramount Theatre: first the movie, then the orchestra. We climbed the staircases curving to the stars under the enormous chandelier of the gilded scarlet entry hall and waited for Jimmy Dorsey or Gene Krupa, Louis Armstrong, Benny Goodman, Harry James, or our lover boy, "Ol' Blue Eyes" Sinatra. We screamed and stomped in the aisles until it was time to run around the corner and board the three o'clock bus to Ridgefield. We'd played hooky and had to forge our mothers' signatures on notes for class the next day.

My ideas about race, national origin, and religion intensified with time to become political statements. At their core is a trait I could only have inherited from my mother, who treated every human being in the same warm, unprejudiced way. I was only a child when her antiracist principles were driven home to me with an iron thrust. We were at Uncle Ralph's in Great Barrington for Thanksgiving—a dozen adults and children around the long dining-room table—when Uncle Ralph called for the *shvartze* to bring in the next dish from the kitchen. His sister, my mother, jumped up and yelled: "Ralph, if you utter that word once more, I'm leaving and you'll never see my face again."

My father, on the other hand, indulged in all the racist epithets: Italians were dagos or wops, Spaniards were spics, and Jews were goddamn Jews if not kikes. When my mother would snap, "Don't say that, Charlie," he would reply, "I don't mean anything by it." One day during the war, he arrived to open the shop and found JEW written in big letters on the store window. He was enraged, but swallowed his anger. Who to complain to? Anti-Semitism was as American as apple pie back then.

The German barber, who'd had a shop on Catoonah Street for as long as anyone could recall, found NAZI scrawled on his window the same day.

In September 1945, I left for college in Georgia. I was sixteen and I was witless. I was heading for the racist, Bible Belt South, to a women's college, Wesleyan. I knew no one who had been to college or intended to go. Even my teachers had only been to two-year normal schools. In a magazine I found a list of all-women's colleges. I applied to five or six and received two positive replies: Vassar and Wesleyan. I judged Vassar too sophisticated, a place for society girls. It was also more expensive. So Wesleyan it was.

I traveled alone by train, twenty-four hours sitting up. With my sleeveless light-wool red dress, a wide-brimmed brown hat, high heels, and stockings, I felt spiffy. Someone took a photo of me on Main Street in Ridgefield as I waited for the bus to New York Penn Station. It was baking hot in Macon and my swell clothes were not appropriate. In front of the college, students in cotton dresses and sandals were on hand to help the new arrivals. In the freshman dorm I met big, blonde Jean Sloane from Chicago, my roommate and one of the few northerners there.

That year turned out to be an education in life, if not in the classics. In the North, I had watched Blacks be invisible, relegated to side doors and homes along the tracks, but segregation was something else, in your face twenty-four hours a day, and its rules were laws. Restrooms, restaurants, public schools, transportation, drinking fountains—all were legally segregated, with signs to warn you who could drink or piss where. It took no time for me to become defiant. I made coffee for the Black maid and helped her clean the room. I sat in the back of the bus or offered the seat next to me to a Black passenger. Off-campus, I was part of a small group that became friends with a left-wing photographer we met one afternoon in a bar. We dropped into his studio on Saturdays and, over drinks, talked about the South and segregation, the Civil War, its history, and our expectations.

The school was strictly Methodist and abstinent. It may well have been the oldest chartered women's college in the world; it was incapable of looking beyond its history. The Second World War had just ended. The Civil War, barely eighty years behind us, remained invasive in subtle ways: northerners were treated like foreign guests who displayed strange accents, ungraceful gestures, and uncivil behavior. We didn't drawl, we spouted. We didn't sidle, we strode. Very few of the women had traveled north; even fewer had visited New York City. The women came from the four corners of Georgia, but they all knew each other. Class and history restrained them from going for more.

The South seemed to me not only racist but underdeveloped economically and inbred culturally. It moved at another pace, it had the dour smell of the past. I made friends, mostly of the "gung-ho" variety. Some drank. With others, I slipped out to date soldiers from a nearby army base waiting to be released from duty. We sneaked in and out at will, went to Atlanta, danced and partied.

One night near the end of the school year, I was dragged from my bed at the midnight hour to attend a special session of the student council with the dean. On the agenda of that meeting: me. Whatever discussion there was had already taken place. I had not sat down before the dean announced, "We don't want you back!"

Startled, I shouted, "I have no intention of coming back. I've had enough of this place!" More calmly, she added, on a final note of hypocrisy: "There'll be nothing in writing."

The faces of the council members, some of whom I had laughed with through the year, were censorious, self-righteous, and closed. There was no eye contact. They were repudiating me in the dark of night.

In the fall of 1946, I enrolled in the two-year Spanish translation program at the Latin American Institute in Manhattan. The teaching staff was composed of refugees from Republican Spain and exiles from fascist regimes in Latin America. Many of the students were World War II vets on the GI Bill. They were older, more aware and political. One day they brought in a speaker from the world-government movement who talked about peace, democracy, and justice on a global scale: "No more wars!" he shouted. We roared with approval. The meeting was a raging success and half the school joined the organization, the United World Federalists.

I had seen friends off to war. I had known men who never returned. Many a time with school friends from Ridgefield, I had driven to a railroad station on the New York Central line to accompany a draftee or an enlisted soldier or sailor from our high school whose furlough had come to an end, poignant separations on a platform in the dusk of early evening, with men in uniform: "We're shipping out in a few days . . ."

The world government meeting, in a matter of minutes, had propelled me into the future. I saw myself marching for peace, joining the battle for freedom from war and injustice. Suddenly, I had an ideal that coincided with my time of life and the historical moment. I wanted to express it.

I paid several visits to the movement offices to pick up literature to distribute at LAI. I got to know members of the staff. After graduating at the end of 1948, I mustered the courage to volunteer at the movement's offices. My political knowledge was sketchy, but I knew how to type—fast—and take shorthand—slowly. I spoke Spanish and had a smattering of French, and I was wired for work and camaraderie. I was welcomed on board and given a short stipend. I was just twenty.

We pursued an agenda of peace, an end to wars hot or cold. We were organizers. In 1950, I was named director of the Student Division. I traveled to schools and universities, made speeches, maintained contacts with other student and youth groups. We were one of the most popular pressure groups on campuses throughout the country. Some UWF supporters were well known: Norman Cousins, William O. Douglas, Mark Van Doren, Bertrand Russell, Oscar Hammerstein, Albert Einstein. Our aim was to influence Congress to advocate the establishment of a world federal government.

My Federalist colleague Nancy Tucker and I joined two other women in an apartment on Sixth Avenue between 12th and 13th Streets, an extended duplex that had been a speakeasy in the '20s.

We placed our beds in front of the stage on the upper floor. The apartment had high ceilings and a series of rooms on the lower floor, containing an upright piano, colorful wallpaper—yellowed and peeling—and battered couches. It was a little seedy, all the more to our liking, and a great place for parties.

I believe we were all virgins, or close to it. Sex activity at the time was called petting, and we certainly partook. Our partners were respectful of the unspoken boundaries; we were in safe hands. Then one day I crossed the line. I believe my roommates were miffed: I had left the club. My lover was an older man, also a colleague but not one of our crowd. I saw him on and off; he would call late at night and pick me up for a drink before going to his place.

For me, the sex was not the high point. In fact, it wasn't the point at all: I wasn't aroused. I didn't know that sex was multifarious and required participation. It would take a while. What I wanted was the older man, wiser and more experienced, a father figure, as I now see it. I was unsure of who I was and where I was going. The same was true for my roommates. We were idealists and we had goals: we were part of the struggle for a better world. We were also insufferable, convinced we had received the "word" and were anointed to spread it. Of course, we never shut up.

Our work was exhilarating but also contained some jolts given the realities of the era: open prejudice against women, Jews, Blacks, and foreigners. On a trip to Des Moines, Iowa, I spoke at the university and met with the local "adult" chapter of the Federalists. I had traveled by train from New York and missed the connection in Chicago. The next train south was a local to Ames, Iowa, where I took to the highway and hitchhiked. I was aware of the dangers, but arriving on time at the university was my overriding concern. It outweighed the risks.

The middle-aged man who stopped for me was driving a small pickup truck and at some point decided to leave the road for the woods. When I started screaming and pounding on him, he turned back and drove me in silence the rest of the way to Des Moines. An unsettling experience, certainly, but no more so than the conversation with the president of the local UWF chapter, a respected businessman, who warned me against sending New Yorkers on speaking trips to his area. "Their names sound foreign," he explained, "and in our part of the country, that can be a put-off." It took me a while to absorb his meaning: people with Jewish-sounding names.

The late 1940s and early 1950s were unsettling times: we were barely out of the hot war before a cold war was under way. Harry Truman championed the Red Scare, replete with security checks, FBI empowerment, loyalty oaths, and trials. Writers and intellectuals were branded eggheads and treated with disdain. Well-loved progressives like Paul Robeson and Howard Fast were refused passports. J. Edgar Hoover's investigators and infiltrators were everywhere: in Hollywood, within the press, and in any organizations advocating friendship or entente, in addition to the Communist Party and its affiliate organizations. Racism and anti-Semitism were given full rein, culminating in the execution of Ethel and Julius Rosenberg in 1953. Hoover demanded censorship and the destruction of books by authors of whom he disapproved. Crowds jeered at progressives: "Kill a commie for Christ!" The idealism of the war years faded away.

It was during that period that FBI agents appeared in Ridgefield asking questions about me—specifically, I was told, about my comments concerning "Negroes." In the summer of 1951, I had attended the World Assembly of Youth (WAY) congress at Cornell University, which brought together delegations of young people from all over the world, except the Communist bloc. I was openly denunciatory on the subject of racism in the United States. Why keep it under raps, I felt. Ithaca, New York, may have been in the non-segregated North, but racism was no less rampant there, simply less visible and regulated. And our guests, among whom were many delegates from Africa, wanted and needed to know what our politics were. One of my colleagues on the US delegation said that he had been approached by an agent asking questions about me.

The Federalist credo was "Peace is not merely the absence of war, but the presence of justice, of law, of order—in short, of government and the institutions of government." What had started as a straightforward proposal—a world federal government to ensure peace among nations and provide solutions to the world's problems—became, with time, more complicated and divisive. A right and a left developed, with the left quartered in the Student Division and the right among the so-called adults. In reaction to attacks from extremists like Senator Joseph McCarthy, who claimed world government was the equivalent of world communism, the main body of the organization downscaled its program to "strengthening" the United Nations through international law, not only avoiding the term "world government" but in effect eviscerating the concept.

For the Student Division, the concern was freedom at home and abroad. Social revolutions against colonialism, feudalism, and poverty were sweeping the world: China, Indochina, India, Malaysia, Korea. The Second World War had just ended and the two superpowers were already heading toward armed confrontation. Immanuel Wallerstein, the future sociologist and world-systems theoretician, became our group's ideological leader—defining a policy of anti-colonialism, international cooperation and development, and détente, as well as the preservation and strengthening of freedom at home, where the effects of the Red Scare and McCarthyism were devastating.

The divisions between UWF's young idealists and its centrist community leaders became more and more pronounced. A split developed at its 1951 national convention that became unbridgeable. The Student Division was thrown out of the organization and I was fired. In December, a few days after my twenty-third birthday, with my Federalist colleague Bill Friedlander, I boarded the good ship Veendam for a stormy, vomitous two-week trip on the high seas to Rotterdam, then Paris, where this story begins.

Acknowledgements

A number of people have contributed to the existence of this book. I would like to name and embrace them: Zeynep Celik, Bell Chevigny, Anne Gehris, Jeremy Harding, Amara Lakhous, Gloria Loomis, Stephanie Love, Marie-Jeanne Manuellan, Samuel Metz, Doreen Rappaport, Adam Shatz, Elena Sheehan, and Perry Winston. Without Mokhtar Mokhtefi's strength and support, I would not have written my story, nor be the person I am.

Notes

1 Post-War Paris

1 Adam Nossiter, *The Algeria Hotel* (New York: Houghton Mifflin, 2001).
2 In the sixties, the bridge and the neighborhood were gutted and redesigned. Tourist hotels now line the Seine; office towers and a large shopping mall have replaced the old Arab quarter. The *dansing* is long gone.

2 The Algerian War

1 Pierre Bourdieu and Abdelmalek Sayad, *Le déracinement. La crise de l'agriculture traditionnelle en Algérie* (Paris: Minuit, 1964).
2 Alistair Horne, *A Savage War of Peace* (New York: New York Review of Books Classics, 1977).
3 Catherine Simon, *Algérie, les années pieds-rouges* (Paris: La Découverte, 2009).
4 *El Watan*, Algiers, September 21, 2017.
5 In 1993, Barbara Malley and I visited Abdelkader in Geneva as he lay dying of cancer, sprawled out on a chaise longue in the middle of his living room. He had lost none of his bonhomie, laughing with us over episodes we had experienced

together in the old office on 46th Street. A month later, he was gone.

6 In 1959, Andrei Gromyko, the Soviet foreign minister, commented that "the Soviet Union's restraint in matters pertaining to Algeria may not have been properly noticed in France." See Mathew Connelly, *A Diplomatic Revolution: Algeria's Fight for Independence and the Crisis of the Post-Cold War Era* (New York: Oxford University Press, 2002).

7 Krim Belkacem was murdered in a hotel room in Frankfurt, Germany, on October 18, 1970, shortly after a failed attempt on Houari Boumediene's life.

8 Ali Boumendjel, FLN lawyer and brother of Ahmed Boumendjel, was tortured and executed by French General Paul Aussaresses and his men in March 1957. Thrown from the sixth floor of a building, his death passed off as suicide. In 2000, Aussaresses admitted having cold-bloodedly tortured and summarily executed dozens of Algerian prisoners, including Boumendjel.

9 Jay Lovestone, a founder of the US Communist Party who later opposed Stalin and, with Irving Brown, founded the International Confederation of Free Trade Unions. Ms. Morris was Lovestone's companion and agent. Norman Thomas was the former leader of the Socialist Party and its presidential candidate until 1948.

10 Quoted in John T. Shaw, *JFK in the Senate* (New York: Palgrave Macmillan, 2013), 104.

11 The term *pied-noir*, or "black-foot," is the tag applied to the European settlers in Algeria. There are various explanations for the term, one being that they arrived barefoot on Algerian soil.

12 Jean Khalfa and Robert Young, eds, *Frantz Fanon. Ecrits sur l'aliénation et la liberté* (Paris: Éditions La Découverte, 2015). Translation is my own.

13 Claude Lanzmann, *Le lièvre de Patagonie* (Paris: Gallimard, 2009).

14 Josie Fanon committed suicide on July 13, 1989, from the balcony of her apartment in a suburb of Algiers.

15 Mohammed Harbi, "Afterword," in Frantz Fanon, *Les damnés de la terre* (Paris: La Découverte/Poche, 2002). Translation is my own.

3 Moving to Algeria

1 Mohamed Benyahia died on May 3, 1982, while on a peace mission to Iran and Iraq, which were at war. His plane was downed by a missile presumed launched by an Iraqi military plane, although never proven absolutely. Much mystery and many conspiracy theories surround this tragic event.

2 In 2001, Henri Pouillot, a soldier stationed at the Villa during the war, paid witness on French TV to the torture Algerian women were subjected to, which included sexual abuse and forced prostitution of militants arrested and women simply pulled off the street.

3 *Le Monde*, June 19, 1965.

4 Fidel Castro, speech to the 9th World Youth and Student Festival, Havana, Cuba, June 1965, lanic.utexas.edu.

4 Meeting the Black Panthers

1 I learned many years later, through the Freedom of Information Act, that this trip to Cuba was the signal event that placed me on the FBI list of persons under surveillance.

2 Fidel Castro, speech finalizing the OLAS Conference, August 11, 1967, lanic.utexas.edu/project/castro.

3 COINTELPRO was created by the FBI in 1956 to disrupt the activities of the US Communist Party. It was expanded in the 1960s to include, among others, the Ku Klux Klan, the Socialist Workers' Party, and the Black Panther Party. COINTELPRO operations were officially terminated on April 28, 1971, shortly after the split in the BPP.

4 See US Senate Select Committee on Intelligence, Church Committee Report, Book III, intelligence.senate.gov.

5 Lowell Bergman and David Weir, "Revolution on Ice," *Rolling Stone*, September 9, 1976.

6 According to Lee Lockwood's *Conversation with Eldridge Cleaver* (London: Jonathan Cape, 1971), Hearne was "mentally disturbed: and claimed that Cleaver had attempted to rape her." In an interview in London (*The Washington Post*, December 10, 1969), Hearne stated that she had been a confidante of Cleaver's and a frequent guest at his apartment in Havana, but fled when he threatened to beat her up.

7 Eric Pace, "Cleaver is Cheered in Algiers as He Denounces Israel as an American Puppet," *New York Times*, July 23, 1969.

8 A group of New York Panthers accused of plotting to blow up department stores, police stations, and commuter railways, charges that were eventually dropped.

9 Negotiations between Sonatrach, Algeria's oil and gas conglomerate, and El Paso Natural Gas Company were well underway. Deliveries of Algerian natural gas to the east coast of the United States would commence in 1974.

5 New Arrivals

1 David Hilliard and Lewis Cole, *This Side of Glory* (New York: Little, Brown and Company, 1993).

2 Private communication from DC to the author.

3 David Hilliard and Lewis Cole, *This Side of Glory* (New York: Little, Brown and Company, 1993).

4 Through the Freedom of Information Act, I was able to verify that FBI agents were actively trying to intercept me on departure but lost my trace.

5 Before leaving for New York, I had been in contact with Brazilian professionals in France through Miguel Arraes, the former governor of Pernambuco, who had been living in exile in Algeria since June 1965. Miguel Arraes had been deposed and imprisoned following the fascist military coup of 1964. Released a year later, he sought asylum in France but was refused. Algeria received

Arraes and his family with open arms. He remained there until 1979, when he was granted amnesty and returned to Brazil.

6 *Hijackers*

1 *New York Times*, June 5, 1972.
2 See Brendan I. Koerner, *The Skies Belong to Us* (New York: Broadway Books, 2014).

7 *A Wedding and Its Consequences*

1 El Ghaouti was his *nom de guerre*, Ali Tounsi his real moniker. In 2009, after fifteen years as director of national security, he was shot and killed in cold blood by his assistant in his padded office at police headquarters.
2 Safiya Bukhari, interview (New York: Safiya Bukhari–Albert Nuh Washington Foundation, March 31, 1992).
3 Michael "Cetewayo" Tabor, *Capitalism Plus Dope Equals Genocide*, undated, marxists.org.
4 Yves Antoine, B., Nicole Chapo, Cynthia Horn, Pierre Ristorcelli and his wife Elizabeth White, Andréa Thibault.
5 Eldridge Cleaver, *Soul on Fire* (Waco, TX: Word Books, 1978).
6 Ibid.
7 Ibid.
8 Ibid, p. 151.
9 Hilliard and Cole, p. 129.
10 Personal correspondence from Don Cox, September 18, 1985.
11 Eldridge Cleaver, *Soul on Ice* (New York: Dell Publishing Company, 1968), pp. 97–106.
12 "Exile's Return," *The Nation*, editorial, December 12, 1976.
13 *Newsweek*, March 17, 1975.

8 After Algiers

1 "I am taking the liberty of asking you to intervene with either the President of the Republic or the Minister of the Interior in favor of Miss Elaine Klein, an American who has just learned that she has been interdict in France for several years. She is reproached with being a close collaborator of the Black Panther leader Eldridge Cleaver. The same ban also applied to E. Cleaver and his wife, but was abrogated several months ago by personal decision of the President of the Republic and they both now reside in France following their long sojourn in Algeria."

2 Mokhtar Mokhtefi, *J'étais français-musulman* (Algiers: Éditions Barzakh, 2016).